The embroidery of Boutis, Art and Technique of a Provençal Treasure

Dedicated to:

Céline,
Amélie,
Agathe,
Carole,
Clémence,
Hélène,
Julie,
and to our grandmothers.

Other books on textiles are available from Edisud Publishers (see following page).
For information on all these books, published only in French, write to the following address.

ISBN 2-7449-0145-8
© Sarl Édisud, La Calade, 3120 Route d'Avignon
F–13090 Aix-en-Provence, 2002.
Tél. 04 42 21 61 44 / Fax 04 42 21 56 20
www.edisud.com – e.mail: commercial@edisud.com

March 2002
Printed in U.E.

FRANCINE NICOLLE

The embroidery of Boutis Art and Technique of a Provençal Treasure

Photographs: Jean-Louis AUBERT
Translated by: Katharine HADEN

EDISUD

From Provence

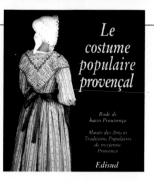

Le Boutis dans le trousseau
Francine Nicolle
Booklet including full size stencils of original and unedited models, created by Francine Nicolle for her book, The Embroidery of Boutis. Advice on the composition and completion attached.
20 x 27 cm. 2 plates. Boxed. © 1999.
ISBN 2-7449-0103-2

Collection « Piquages de Provence »
Boxed booklets (24 x 32 cm) including full size unedited stencils of original drawings and models, created by the author. Sheets with advice on

composition and completion are included.

Fleurs de Boutis
From the flowers in the herb garden to the famous flowers on the provençal printed calicos,

through fantasy flowers, symbols of love, purity or femininity.
ISBN 2-7449-0313-2

Piqués de soie
How to complete and personalise bedspreads, table runners, chair covers or christening 'pétassons'.
ISBN 2-7449-0337-X

Piqués de coton
Show off your talents on bedspreads, counterpanes; play with traditional motifs used to decorate chairs, armchairs and the 'radassiers' of the large country houses.
ISBN 2-7449-0336-1

Symboles dans la broderie au Boutis
Long life and immortality, wealth and prosperity, lineage and descendants, love, religion, career… This box offers a diverse selection of motifs and drawings with the symbolism of the art of the 'boutis' as the central theme. Discover the secret language that made our embroiderers famous, as well as follow the advice given to avoid committing errors.
ISBN 2-7449-0335-3

Piqué de Provence
Counterpanes and printed skirts from the collection of André-Jean Cabanel (18th – 19th century) from the Museum of Fabric Printing, Mulhouse. A reference work which retraces the history, techniques and symbolism of the provençal piqué through pieces of exceptional quality.
24 x 29 cm. 200 p. Hardback with cover. Colour photographs © 2000.
ISBN 2-7449-0158-X

Le Costume populaire provençal
Rode de Basso Prouvenco
This work presents a complete picture of traditional clothing in Provence, cataloguing the costumes and accessories according to their social class and the events of the time.

27 x 29 cm. 224 p. Hardback with cover. Colour illustrations. © 1996.
ISBN 2-85744-500-8

Le Textile en Provence
Annie Roux
With talent, the author retraces the history of making textiles in Provence from the multiple raw materials to the products ready for fashion.
24 x 30 cm. 240 p. Hardback with cover. colour illustrations. © 1994.
ISBN 2-85744-745-0

Histoire singulière de l'impression textile
Museum.f Fabric Printing, Mulhouse
A selection of printed fabric masterpieces, including the most remarkable pieces of their time.
21 x 29.7 cm. 224 p Paperback. Colour photographs. © 2001. ISBN 2-7449-0240-3

L'Etoffe au fil des civilisations
Nicole Renau
Starting with the masterpieces that still exist in museums and official palaces around the world,

the author retraces the magnificent history of fabric: from the first Neolithic weavings to those of the present day; the fascinating progression across the civilisations of the East and West with the fabric becoming either more personnel or more ostentatious.
24 x 29 cm. 208 p. Hardback. © 2000. ISBN 2-7449-0151-2

Costumes du Maroc
Jean Besancenot
Including minutely detailed sketches of sixty costumes, this work offers a unique testament to the culture and the traditions of a now distinct Morocco.
New Edition 2000 – New presentation in a smaller size. Complete text with illustrations. 24 x 27,5 cm. 176 p. Hardback with cover. © 2000. ISBN 2-7449-0218-7

Au fil du désert
Tents and fabric of the Mediterranean nomadic shepherds
Arnaud Maurières, C. Lapeyrie, Eric Ossart

Around one hundred pieces of textiles characteristic of the nomadic life in the Mediterranean, representing the diverse tribes of Syria, Libya, Neguey, Sinaï and the raised plateau of Maghreb…
21 x 29.7 cm. 120 p. Paperback. Colour, and Black and White illustrations. © 1996. ISBN 2-85744-806-6

Maroc, tapis de tribus
H. Crouzet, C. Bouilloc, A. Maurières, M.-F. Vivier
21 x 29.7 cm. 160 p. Paperback. Colour illustrations. © 2001. ISBN 2-7449-0155-5

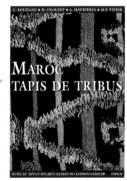

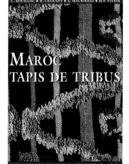

Tazra, bijoux et tapis de Ouarzazate
Anne Barthélémy
This book evokes the traditional arts of the silversmith and the weaver of the high Atlas mountains in the confines of the Dra and the Dadès, taken from extremely fine drawings created by her father in the 1930s.
25 x 32 cm. 128 p. Hardback with cover. Colour, and Black and White illustrations. © 1990. ISBN 2-85744-498-2

Afrique bleue, les routes de l'indigo
Museum of Clermont-Ferrand
Catalogue created at the time of the exhibition 'Afrique bleue, les routes de l'indigo' organised by the Museum of Rugs and Textile Arts in Clermont-Ferrand.
21 x 29.7 cm. 160 p. Paperback. © 2000. ISBN 2-7449-0209-8

Algéroises, histoire d'un costume méditerranéen
Leyla Belkaïd
The author invites us to travel in the footsteps of Algerian traditional costumes, its history and its functions in the social and cultural life of the country.
24 x 30 cm. 192 p. Hardback with cover. Colour and Black and White illustrationso © 1998. ISBN 2-85744-918-6

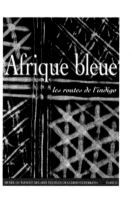

Contents

Preface

In an age when change is so rapid, it is fortunate that certain people know that to keep balance and identity it is important to conserve or even rediscover the footprints from the past, to rekindle a past still alive in the memory of our elders. This wish is not only – in fact far from it – that of the authorities and their policy to defend their heritage, but also that of the local people whose demonstrated taste for antiques and their conservational actions play an important role in the real renaissance of this precious heritage. This book is the evidence.

It is not the first book to deal with the 'boutis': two pieces of fabric sewn together by 'broderie emboutie' following a method derived from the 'piqué de Marseille' whose motifs represent the group symbolic. For example, the work of the American Kathryn Berenson on the 'piqué' and the Provencal 'boutis', and of Andrée Gaussens from the Auvergne whose book entitled *Manuel du Boutis* informs us of the technical approach, already uncover the 'boutis'. This book was also studied by a group of student ethnologists at the Paul Valéry University, Montpellier, in the context of an investigation under my direction, handling 'Ethnology and Cultural Heritage'. Francine Nicolle, the child of an old Vaunage family, brings another view: that of an erudite collector who considers the 'boutis' as a female legacy that she discovers at the heart of the thoughtfully designed Languedocien and Provencal trousseau.

All these authors owe a lot to other women, to the antique dealers of old 'boutis' – yellowed fabrics splendidly embroidered but marked with stains from the linen cupboard – which they generally trade in, and who say themselves that they like "the linen and the merchandise of women". What they sell most frequently are pillowcases, 'pétassons' or 'bourrassons' – small squares which served to carry the baby – and 'vanes', bedspreads of which the oldest are priceless. As for 'jupons', they are the hardest to find, and even more rare, as they were often transformed into 'pétassons'.

Collectors of 'boutis' search in particular for the 'jupon'. They are looking to return this to the society where it was largely used: the Bas-Languedoc of the 18th and 19th centuries. One of the interesting points Francine Nicolle is to introduce us to is of two female collective work-groups, those of Vauvert and Marsillargues, and to extract from their study some pertinent questions: how to explain the very neat differences between the productions of these two work-groups despite the fact that they are neighbours? This is the beginning of an enquiry that would be interesting to continue in the area of manufacture of the 'boutis' in the Bas-Languedoc.

The 'jupon' appears as a 'fait total' in the sense that Marcel Mauss gave the expression. "We did it for life," we said, and, in fact, the embroidered 'jupon' participates in the cycle of life, 'from marriage to birth' - to use the expression of Francine Nicolle. A 'jupon' embroidered by a young girl becomes the 'jupon' of the bride; second-hand, it is the clothing of the newborn and also the shroud of the dead. The solidity of the 'boutis' and the 'piqué' as well as their long term re-use explains why they were handed down within the same family like a wardrobe with the other parts of the trousseau: jewels 'dorures' and 'verdure': the real estate of ground. This rich person's fabric has become, with the passing of time, also the poor girl's fabric who learnt to embroider in order to earn a living in the work-group or by the passing down of family knowledge. These girls dressed themselves in this way, from simple cotton at little cost to a prestigious manner for a long period of time.

The 'boutis', and this is not the least of its interests, is a female script, 'little pointers of the past': women recounting their lives. Francine Nicolle approaches this essential aspect in the chapter 'Motifs and symbols' where she shows how these women presented themselves with the initials of their name; how they spoke of their husband, of his profession, the happy and sad moments, embroidering the cypress as a sign of mourning, flowers as a sign of love, grapes as a sign of wealth, scallop shells as a sign of pilgrimage…

As a document, work of art, feminine prose, product of the languedoc, creation of our elders, witness of our local heritage, the 'boutis' merits what Francine Nicolle and her friends of the Association "Les Cordelles boutis en Vaunage" wish to give it a museum.

Jocelyne BONNET
Teacher of Ethnology
Montpellier University III

Introduction

The 'boutis' has made a prisoner of me. As with Ariadne, I am trying in my own way to unravel the thread that leads me to the source of truth, for the 'boutis' is an enigma and the few pieces of information on this subject do not permit the haloed mystery to be pierced.

"To fall in love" through books with an art barely glimpsed in childhood at a grandmother's house who had the occasion to sell 'vanes' and dreamy 'jupons' is somewhat odd! Is this glance of a small child etched in my memory to the point that at a given moment the sparkle needed to re-appear? Why was it necessary that one day, from the force of memory, I felt irresistibly liable for generations of grandmothers I didn't know at all and who were yet so close at the same time?

Nothing predisposed me to this research, to go back in time in search of answers. The transmission of these ladies' gestures with all that they convey of traditions, but on which there are few words written, are passed on by the understanding of the way of living, by the daily rituals and by the turning of the seasons. On each side of the Rhone almost precisely the same ways of doing things exist, but with such slight differences.

In the period of Louis XIV, there was not a single written word on the different aspects of the techniques of the 'boutis'. Charles Germain de Saint-Aubin, embroiderer to the King, explained in his work, *'L'art du brodeur'*, a great many forms of embroidery, but he spoke little on 'boutis'; his citations are scattered and do not permit a good understanding of this particular type of stitched embroidery. So it is necessary to fill in certain gaps. At the present time, trade is seized by the pretty word of 'boutis' and is profiting from the confusion that is created - the fault of an over-precise vocabulary. Under the charm of this magical word, a number of padded 'courte-pointes' are able to seduce an uninformed clientele who are conquered immediately by the ancestral home-made techniques which not only evoke southern France, but make one dream of skies forever blue…

I have been given the opportunity to bring together a whole combination of observations and information that I have put in order, during systematic research. A teacher by profession, I have used all forms of investigation: surveys on the ground, interviews, documentations, libraries, heritage collections, county archives. The 'boutis' studied were quite literally put under a microscope, on a lit-cold table in order to be radiographed. All the designs were noted, analyzed and given a place by comparison, which enabled a table of frequency to be created. Each boutis had its own personal form. All the technical details were catalogued, as were the materials used.

The first thing to do was to re-find the technique, the mastering of the technique: without this, it would not be possible to find sensible explanations, but at the same time, from studying the movement of the hand, if it brought answers, it would also throw up more questions. From a long and practical study of the 'boutis', I could hypothesize, have an intuition, and then check it out on the ground, that is to say, on the old 'boutis'. Moreover, the ways of learning, the questions posed, the interest manifested by the people whom I have had the pleasure of teaching the 'boutis', considerably advanced things. The age of my pupils varies from 6 to 83; all the generations that have desired to learn this popular art have discovered the magic and the undeniable beauty that springs from it. I have had the immense satisfaction of seeing works of a very high standard executed, and all that from beginners' lessons on 'boutis'. In schools, high schools and colleges, young people have discovered works and tools totally unknown to them, and one after another dissolved in pleasure at the relief modeled by their fingers.

The collection studied has many origins. First and foremost they come from old women – rooted in the Gard for many generations – who happily opened their doors to me and entrusted me with their 'boutis' in order that I might study them. Their secrets, particularly moving, contributed to the modification of the way I perceived this popular art. These 'boutis' were original: handed down from one generation to the next, the majority of the time not even leaving the walls of their 'birth'. From the beginning of this adventure, two collectors from the region agreed to participate in

exhibitions, and put rare pieces in my care. It is because of them that I have been able to embark on this long snail's-pace work. I thank most warmly all the lenders, known or unknown, without whom this task would not have had the same range.

As a little girl, from the age of 11, I picked grapes for the table and the harvest in order to help buy my schoolbooks. In amongst the vines I was no taller than the vine stumps! I was 'worth' only half as much as an adult, but I worked as hard as an adult. Like the olive tree and the crook of the herdsman, the bunch of grapes is an important symbol of the Southern French region. It manifests the traditions and the way of life in the Midi.

"Madame de Maintenon embroidered everywhere, and in every place,
during coach journeys and during council with the King."
On her cart taking her to Beauvoisin, Mira was stitching her small 'couverton'…
In the TGV (high speed train) or on a plane, I 'boutisse' Julie's 'vanon'…

History
and techniques

*The lords' residences appreciated the wall hangings and the 'courtepointes'. The scenes taken from the Bible like **"The chastity of Joseph"** or **"The dish found in Benjamin's bag"** served as themes for printed fabrics.*

History

Dream legends

Troubadours sang of marvellous legends in the courtyards of the greats in this world, giving birth to the West and engendering dreams of travelling. Some, more than others, registered in the imagination of men. The lives of strange people became an inexhaustible source of fabulous stories told by word of mouth, and reproduced afterwards by needle on sheets of white fabric. In order to immortalize them forever in the memory of man by illuminations of another kind, thread replaced ink, the wadding of wool gave birth to the original colour palettes in which the nuance of light and shade permitted the creation of embroidery, which would be extremely popular in the 13th century. Called by the pretty name of 'broderie en rondes-bosses', this new technique made visible by relief, between the two layers of fabric, the heroes evolving in their framework of life. The 'broderie en bosses'[1] sculpted the fabric with delicacy and intelligence. The relief of shape gave life to the events of stories that would enchant whole generations.

It is in this way that the first history books and novels, both romantic and adventure, were born under the fingers of Sicilian embroiderers. The written traces of the sewing thread will tell with incredible precision epics that have crossed centuries, and which - even now - still make us dream.

In the past, Sicily was the quilting workshop of the Early Middle Ages[2]. In this place of transit for the crusaders, many civilisations disgorged onto the island the habits and customs of other continents. During the course of the Crusades,[3] cultural and commercial exchanges multiplied. Precious objects, the richest of silks and the most sparkling fabrics were transported via the same routes.

The life of King Solomon, known for his wisdom and his sense of justice, and also that of Alexander the Great, are given as examples on the 'courtepointes' mentioned in 1426 in an inventory of Baux Castle in Provence.

The most famous of these legends sung by the troubadours dates from the 14th century. It is of Celtic origin. It tells of the impossible love between Tristan and Isolde, finally united, but only in death. This marvellous story was recounted by needle on a counterpane originating from Sicily. It is embroidered 'from the inside' and is dated 1395. Fourteen pictures, similar to the pages of a book, recount the events that determined the path of these two lovers and give form to the silhouettes of the characters evolving around the heroes. Armour, faces and castles are underlined with great precision. The details of the fingers, the characteristics of the clothes, demonstrate the care put into the work to ensure a perfect likeness. Another older 'courtepointe' or hanging from the same century also tells this history. It is in England.

Reserved for the professional or most experienced embroiderers, the technique of 'broderie en bosses'[1] was all the rage in the 13th century. These educational themes, telling the lives of real people, aroused the admiration of a dazzled audience, and became the inexhaustible sources of works of art for the whole of the Decorative Arts.

A perfume from abroad

The *Livre des Merveilles* relates to Marco Polo's journey across Asia from 1271 to 1296. It is one of the great successes of the Middle Age. First written in German in 1477, it was later translated into Italian and then French. The stories of twenty-five years of discoveries, with illustrations, interested the greatest sailors who made a point of reading them before leaving for the same destinations.

Even earlier – since antiquity – spices and precious objects had been traded throughout the Mediterranean. Following the silk route, caravans loaded with fabrics reached the ports of Aleppo, Alexandria, Smyrna, and then by sea routes, on large caravels, the goods made their entrance into the port of Marseilles. In the trading posts of the Levant, the quilted fabrics covered both the ground and the cradles of the newborn. The Midi area of France maintained the close commercial ties with the powerful Italian cities and the Mediterranean region.

Fabrics stitched with silk covered the floors and beds in the caravanserai from the East.

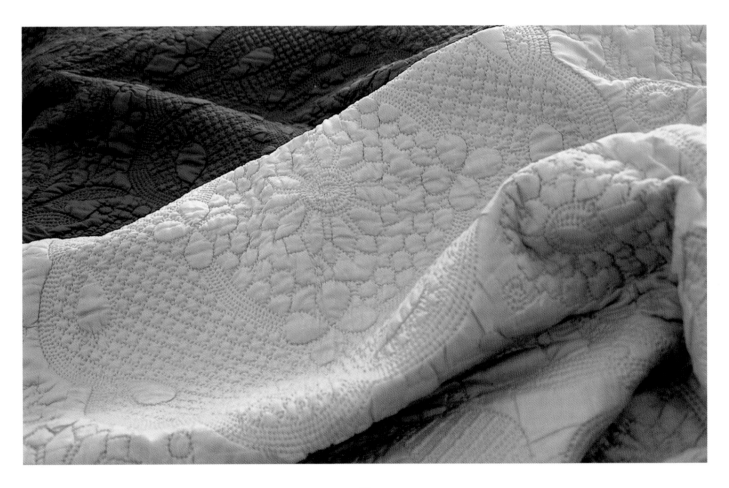

The spirit of India

In the 13th century, the world began to move. The Indian spice route, overland, marked by Alexander the Great, became the goal and dream of the great explorers, and especially of their commanders who were the kings of the European countries. The myth of the Indian spice route, by sea, was also to be realised. Sailors entertained the maddest of plans: to return with their holds full of riches, gold, spices, precious woods, luxury fabrics. The Portuguese Bartolomeo Diaz, in 1488, rounded the Cape of Good Hope, and Christopher Columbus discovered America in 1492, but it was Vasco da Gama who, after many difficulties, reached Calcutta in 1498. The spice route was finally established. The Portuguese, who kept a monopoly on trade with India for a long time, noted the importance of the Italians as well as the Muslims whilst there.

In the eyes of the public, everything exotic came only from great distances, from India, from China… Amongst the treasures shown at Bordeaux during the exhibition "The Spice Route" in 1998, a large hanging in 'broderie emboutie' was a huge success. Of large dimensions (376 cm x 325 cm) made in ivory coloured silk on the right side and emerald cotton on the back, this piece dates from approximately the 16th century. Its make-up relates moments of the lives of the Lords of that period: a hunting scene both with real European animals and fantasy animals, just as, at the base, a naval battle contrasts with Turkish and European pavilions. Its composition is perfect, a balanced centre underlined with a surround of arches that were then in fashion on European tapestries. The faces of the decorated hunters are not of a white race; in this way, the precision of the thread permitted such distinctions and was able to play the role of photography. In the corners of this work of art, two eagles are shown, taking the place of the signatures of the commanders. It is a matter of either a Royal or Imperial house, of Italy or Portugal. Other hangings of this type exist, of identical quality, from India, from the Malabar or Coromandel Coast. The stitching used in both cases is miniscule and clearly marks the contours of each character or element represented. The same technique unites two pieces of different origins: Sicily and India.

However, the Sicilian technique precedes the Indian technique. It is therefore within the Mediterranean that it is necessary to look for the origins of these techniques.

A breeze from the Orient

Nevertheless it is towards Syria that our attention should fall because it is there that cotton named the 'magic plant' is at the origin of the 'samdeh'. Here, to this day, is the oldest of imprints of which we are aware, which mentions the two layers of material, stitches, stuffed inside with cotton, in order to give a relief with meaning. In the book, *Syrie, signes d'étoffes*, Mustapha Fathi has shared his knowledge. He is interested in fabrics printed in his country, and has studied boards carved with motifs of which he is hoping to re-find the meaning. At this time, he recalls the 'samdeh'. The 'samdeh' is made by the hunter; it is a talismanic work consisting of two layers of cotton on which he has reproduced, with the help of stitching, his own hunting territory. A real map, certain areas are stuffed inside with absorbent cotton; the hiding places where the game is found are not quilted, allowing the light through the transparency. Understanding the 'samdeh' is impossible, except by the hunter himself. The secret code transcribed on the fabric, creating links between use, meaning and human relation, already bear witness to the intimate rapport that unites man to textile.

With the opening of new trade routes, Christian Europe confirmed its identity. In India, the Mogul kings, curious to know other forms of thinking, and fascinated by Western Art, received a Jesuit mission in 1580. These first travellers welcomed in India since Marco Polo felt an intense emotion at the sight of the countless riches held in the palaces of the Indian princes. The mixture of styles, the exchange of illustrations, the thirst for new things and the need to appropriate different techniques would permit both economic and cultural growth.

The taste for the exotic aroused new desires and Louis XIV created the 'Compagnie des Indes' in 1664 and then the 'Compagnie du Levant' in 1670, courtesy of his minister Colbert. The consummation of fabrics became the centre of an up and coming activity, which would soon be established around the large French ports.

Colbert's signature

Magnificent Marseilles

When did this tradition of quilting techniques re-surface in the South of France? From the arrival of cotton en masse in Marseilles and especially the arrival of painted fabrics from India or the East, the economy of the entire region changed. It was the beginning of European printing. From 1640[4], Marseilles threw itself into the production of printed calico, copying those from India. The success was immediate, with the colours, its value for money and easy upkeep seducing the population. As a result, the pressure from the draper and the silk manufacturers of Lyons intensified; the royal power ordered a ban on importation, on the fabrication and usage of printed fabrics. It was Louvois, minister to Louis XIV, who put forward the first decree in 1686[5]. Free port since 1669, Marseilles escaped the ban, but had difficulty in distributing its cotton production throughout the kingdom. Despite the contraband which appeared and which gave rise to severe sanctions in the country, thousands of jobs were threatened. The need to find other outlets became imperative. The authorisation to introduce white cloth in the country, "on the condition that it was quilted", would prevent the unemployment that threatened the furniture manufacturers[6]. In order to avoid an economic crisis, the improvement of fabrics by quilting was intensified. With satin and silk being the specialities of the town, there is a strong possibility that this technique was practised long before the arrival of professionally embroidered cotton. The Rhone did not constitute an obstacle to the evolution of these techniques, as the Beaucaire Fair was one of the keystones of the European economy. Everything that came from the North and the Orient passed through it. There is nothing surprising in that, after Italy, the techniques were transported into Provence and the Languedoc, and that they should find a favoured land there. It is enough to refer to the inventories of the time to recognise the point to which the quilted fabrics benefited from a real infatuation, especially in the Midi region of France.

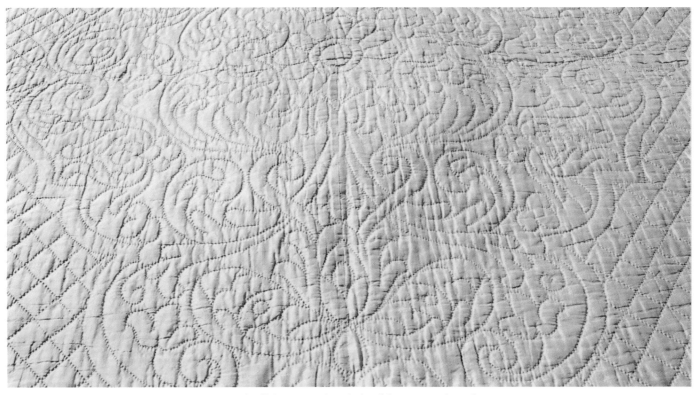

Stately silk 'courtepointe' stitched with large armorial motifs.

Large 'courtepointe' with vibrantly armorial arabesques.

(These documents are shown with the spelling of the period.)

Inventory of François de Calvière, lord of Boissières
(1654 – Arch. Dép. 1j 1082)
- 1 stitched quilted 'vanne', from Cadix
- 4 Flanders tablecloths
- Set of bed linen, from Cadix, with fringes of many amaranth or yellow-blue colours
- Set of bed linen of yellow burasse
- Set of Damascus linen – cover fringe in gold and silver
- Set of linen in yellow taffeta reinforced by 3 fingers + silk fringes
- Tapestries to decorate the bedrooms of Monsieur or Madame
- Coverings for the table or for the floor
- English silk stockings
- Stockings from Cadix
- 'Bazin' bonnets
- 12 tablecloths in 'Cordat'
- Furniture coverings (sheets)
- 'Couverture' in black bourazin

Inventory of Jacques Pieyre, Merchant.
(1744 – Arch. Dép. 2 B 165)
- White stitched skirt… in 'broderie emboutie'…?
- Set of bed linen in stitched yellow taffeta
- Tablecloths in figured fabric
- 'Couverte' in cotton
- 'Couverte in fabric from Montpellier
- 'Couverte' in a painted blue fabric with white dots
- 'Recouverte' of painted fabric and stitched red
- Yellow valance in cotton fabric bordered with blue braid
- Stitched 'couverture' in white satin with yellow flowers and sides in taffeta
- Stitched 'couverte' in chiffon

Possessions of M. Rochemore d'Aigremont
(Emigrant – sale of his estate: 1791-1793)
- 16 feather quilts or 'couvertures'
- 10 green 'aunes'
- 1 printed calico 'vanne' with flowers
- 1 stitched green 'vanne'
- Quilts of stitched fabrics
- Another white stitched 'vanne'
- 2 white 'vannes' of stitched material
- 2 green 'vannes' of stitched material

'Courtepointe' of white basin. The elegant motifs are suggestive of heraldry coats of arms. The stitching is much sought after and imparts a certain nobility to the ensemble.

Techniques

Around the word 'piqué'

The richness of the Occitan language is such that the same word can indicate an object with infinite subtleties, or on the contrary, be different from one region to the next. Here we have 'culachons'[7], somewhere else, 'bourrassons', when in fact we are actually talking about the same thing. The word 'piqué' is remarkable because the number of its applications and meanings is enormous and varied, as everything is stitched, even straw mattresses! It often arises in the notarial vocabulary of the period. It is always associated with silk (*soye*), painted fabrics, printed calico, muslin and especially white 'basin'[8]. In France, the first reference to it in an inventory was in 1653, on a blanket printed with flowers in the Turkish style,[9] stitched on both sides for Mazarin, minister to Louis XIII. In 1660, the Échevins and deputies of Marseille[10] gave the wife of the first assistant to the great Colbert, Madame Bellinzini, three skirts stitched as a present. The inventory of François de Calvière of 1654 mentions a stitched quilted blanket from Cadix[11].

The first classifications became essential in the face of the complexity of different types. It comprises two distinct groups of stitches that we differentiate by:
- The exterior appearance
- The textiles used
- The number of layers of fabrics
- The order of the execution of the technique.

Groupe I	Groupe II
Starting from the stitches, sewing three layers of fabric together with the help of little running stitches, which determine the motifs or lines creating a decoration more or less important.	Starting from the stitches, sewing together two layers of fabric with the help of little stitches enclosing all the elements of an ornamental decoration more or less complicated. The tufts of cotton that give the piece its volume are introduced during the second phase of the work, between the two layers and introduced from the wrong side.

Groupe I

– wadding
– quilting
– some 'trapunto'

Groupe II

– Naples Work
– Florentine stitches
– 'Piqûres de Marseille'
– 'Broderie emboutie'
– 'Broderie de Marseille'
– 'Piqué de Marseille'
– Boutis

All these appellations are classed within the raised embroidery group, and are presented in their chronological order.

'Courtepointe' of coloured silk "baiso ma mio" (the kiss of my beloved) with exceptional stitching.

P 23. Quilted printed calico 'courtepointe' with rich motifs. Before 1806 the green colour was obtained by placing yellow and blue together.

P 24/25. Vibrantly coloured arabesques with the reverse perfectly coordinated for a large 'courtepointe'.

The wadding – stitched works from group 1

Wadding has existed for thousands of years. As with many inventions, it comes from China. A printed and painted dress was found in the tombs of the Hans, in the course of archaeological digs in Northern China. The volume of the stuffing was given by the silk wadding. In ancient times wadding was to be found in central Asia. Its progression follows that of the silk route: present in the nomadic tents of central Europe, then under the armour of the Crusaders, and in Italy where the word 'trapunto' covers several different styles.

Trapunto

It was probably the Crusades that introduced this to Italy. From the workshops in existence since the 13th Century in Sicily, what were the changes that evolved within the technique, and were there any differences? Through the course of an enquiry in Italy, several witnesses brought light to questions that as yet, have no answers.

The encyclopaedia gives the following definition, which has been translated into English:

Trapunto: quilting technique, also called corded quilting, which consists of putting together two pieces of fabric by stitching fine parallel lines through which cotton (cord or cord piping) is inserted. Originally Italian, trapunto was hugely successful in clothing during the 18th century.

The French-Italian dictionary gives some extra pointers:

Trapunta: 'courtepointe', stitch between two layers of fabric.

Trapuntato: padded, the trapunto was in backstitch.

The Italian trapunta are made from three layers (ordinary fabric for the underside – the middle layer of wadding – good quality fabric for the topside). They introduce carefully chosen stitches, based on geometric motifs, pretty garlands, and large stars in the corners. The middle layer was made of silk wadding called "bava" or of wool. The 'courtepointes' in the Midi were square or rectangular, as opposed to the Italian trapunta which had a fold for tucking under the mattress. Also there was 'piqué-bourré' giving a greater raised effect to an important area. Other trapunta appear to introduce an amalgamation of techniques, Marseilles stitching, 'boutis' and padding but all requiring a lining. Padding with tufts of cotton on the underside was done through cut openings that needed to be closed afterwards by sutures. Whereas the most beautiful 'boutis' held their pattern, the underside of the trapunto needed to be lined.

Stitched 'courtepointe' and lined silk 'jupon' backed in bronzed tones. (Photographed at the Musée des Vallées Cevenoles at Saint Jean du Gard).

The splendour of the meridionnal stitching

Marseilles, in its turn, was to distinguish itself by the quality of its stitching, one of its specialties, and achieve worldwide fame. Improvements led to the employment of 2,000 people in fabric, as many in the furniture factories as at home. In inventories from the 17th century onwards the word 'piqué' becomes more frequent. Almost everything that came into contact with the bed was 'piqué'. The finer fabrics were worked on in town and were confined to artists who were the most experienced. Other fabrics were stitched in houses or in the countryside.

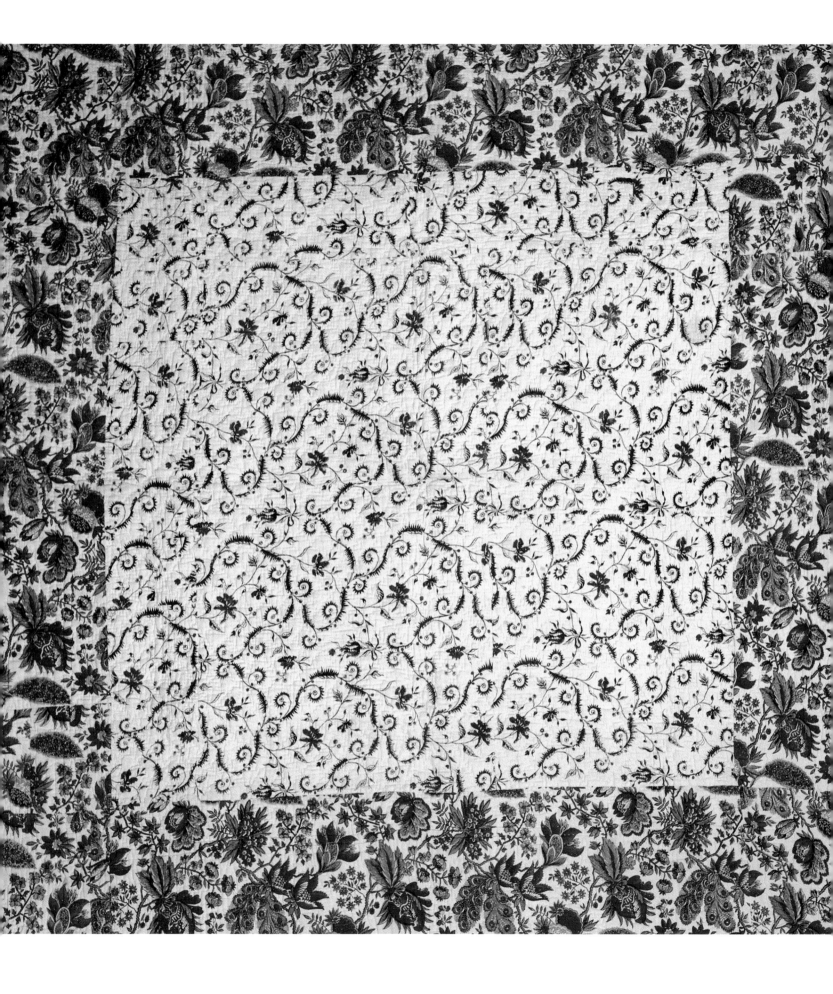

The frame

The most beautiful 'courtepointes' were done on frames. The frame is made of wood, comprising:

– Two large bars of hard wood (chestnut, walnut or a hard white wood) fitted with mortises at each end. A strip of fabric was sometimes nailed onto these bars in order to pin the fabric at its ends. For the 'jupons' and 'cotillons', the bars measured 3.2m.

– The other two bars measured between 1.2m to 1.5m or sometimes more. These were perforated and served to dictate the height of the work with the help of pegs and stretching.

Traditional stitching frame. (Photographed at the Musée des Vallées Cevenoles at Saint Jean du Gard).

Preceding page: Colours and motifs perfectly coordinated on a padded 'vane', printed by a copper roll. From the collection of A.J. Cabanel.

The stitching

In the techniques of group 1, several categories of textile were used, from the most refined to the most common.

The fabrics

– Cotton
– Printed calico with small motifs
– Persian fabrics (printed calico with large motifs)
– Printed calicos of both small and large motifs
– Filoselle
– Silk
– Satin
– Taffeta

The trimmings

– Carded cotton (cotton wadding)
– Silk wadding
– Wool (from the foothills of the lower Alps or the Cevennes)

Cotton centres other than Marseilles developed these techniques: Nimes, Montpellier, Orange, Avignon and the areas around them with art and competence, and in the peripheral villages where the less important work was distributed whilst the luxury products were dealt with in town. The craze for cotton fabrics either plain or patterned was facilitated by their upkeep (washing with soda soap, and no ironing) and the comfort and warmth they afforded were the supplementary assets in favour of their production. The body of the work concerning this stitching is not well defined; the upholsterers, the merchant upholsterers, the taffeta workers, the cotton workers and the 'futainiers' produced 'vanes' and 'courtepointes' which were sold all over France and abroad, including America and the Islands.

This savoir-faire crossed the threshold into homes; stuffing was used in clothes, touching every stratum of society: a stitched silk 'jupon' was worn to Court, under the French style dresses and in regional costume where the piece of mastery remained "lou coutillon pica" (stitched 'cotillons'). From head to toe, padded clothes were to be found thickening or merely livening up clothes or accessories: cloaks, 'corps mous' (hiding the corset), 'casaquins' (housecoat/overall), dressing gowns and nightcaps, parts of clothing, children's' bonnets, bibs…

The search for a relief that was even more pronounced on the garlands and motifs bordering certain 'courtepointes' stems from the technique of 'piqué-bourré' - a word created to illustrate the concept and to emphasize those reliefs that were fuller than others. Having partly stitched the motifs, the tufts of cotton were added with the help of long plant stalks, and then the stitching was finished in order to close off that area which was just packed.

Following page: white jupon (underskirt) with pretty garland motifs and heart shaped vases, and a cotillon (overskirt) of printed flowery calico. Both skirts are wadded.

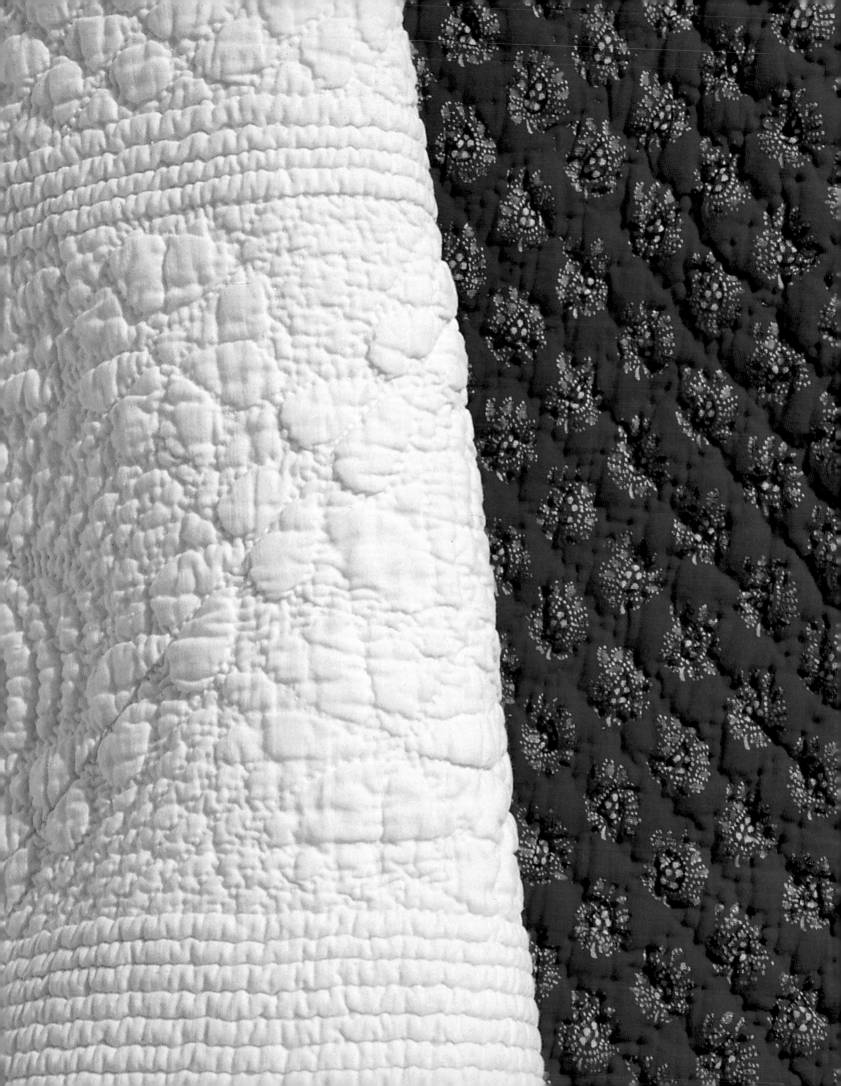

The evidence

The evidence from the doyennes has given life and accuracy to the methods of fabrication that have been lost over time.

Mme Alle, born in 1906 in Calvisson (in Vaunage, near Nîmes), tells:

"My mother in law, Delphine, born in 1884, made stitched 'couvertures' until around 1928. She made the frame herself with four boards and installed herself in the courtyard, in the shade of the mulberry trees. The frame was placed on four chairs. Then stretching the fabric with the help of tacks, she placed a layer of consistently even wadding, then a piece of beautiful fabric on top, which was left loose. Then she hand-stitched the three layers of fabrics during the day using a thick Chinese thread and a large needle choosing running stitches. In the winter, this work was done during the lost time of the day, in the evening, in the kitchen. With a crayon she traced the roses, the garlands and the large leaves. When this work was finished, she removed the 'couverture' and used overcast stitch to complete the edge."

Mme Paulette Delpuech, her friend, confirmed the facts, and tells that at Sumène and at Saint-Bauzile de Putois (Gard), before 1919, she saw (the same pieces) being done in her family but specifies:

"The frame was made to measure; the dimensions varied from one frame to another. The tacks had a flat head, and were not driven all the way in. It was a very long piece of work which unfurled often in the immense kitchen".

What became of the frames? After they had been used, they were burnt.

Marguerite Monestier, born in 1913, tells:

"I am the tenth in a family of twelve children and was married in 1940. I was working; I worked[12] the ground. At 9 years of age, in the summer, I looked after the cows… I didn't go to school very often. I placed myself at the doctors as a domestic. At home I did no sewing other than crochet and stitched 'couvertures'. I still have my frame in the Lozère. It's made of four bars, all longer than the 'couverture'. It was necessary to stretch the fabric to the full. Every 10 centimetres, I placed a tack without driving it in the whole way. In the middle I placed some carded wool in a cross, to equal it out. For the topside I used a single coloured fabric with sheen, stronger than satinette, and also stretched it. I walked all alone to buy it.

I prepared my designs on cardboard; I made templates, always the same, and I drew them with chalk before assembling the whole piece. I had roses, circles, and I traced the lines for the grid.

It was necessary to start at the bottom of the 'couverture'.

I stitched with a thick thread and a large needle. For my part, my stitches were very small. My left hand lifted the taught fabric. It's difficult, of course, to make such small stitches… the stitches were right at the end of our fingertips! There were women who made their 'couvertures' on their knees, but mine, they were the most beautiful! When one area was completed, it was rolled onto the bar, and then we continued.

"We filmed Marguerite as her evidence was worth its weight in gold, her verve did not tire us. Her lively eyes, her mouth, her hands taking up the 'couvertures', these 'couvertures', with the assurance of someone who knows what they are doing, which on the beds, cosseted and pampered the people of her house, the people that she loved.

Whether they were stretched or not, made by professionals or by amateurs, in the towns or in the countryside, as far as the orphanages, the stitching techniques affected the whole population of the lower Occitan region. The types of fabrics used, the ways of making these works, the motifs used and the use within the clothing industry, constitute the elements that permitted a refinement of a regional textile heritage.

Raised perfection (whilst electricity didn't exist… it wasn't widespread until the beginning of the 20th century).

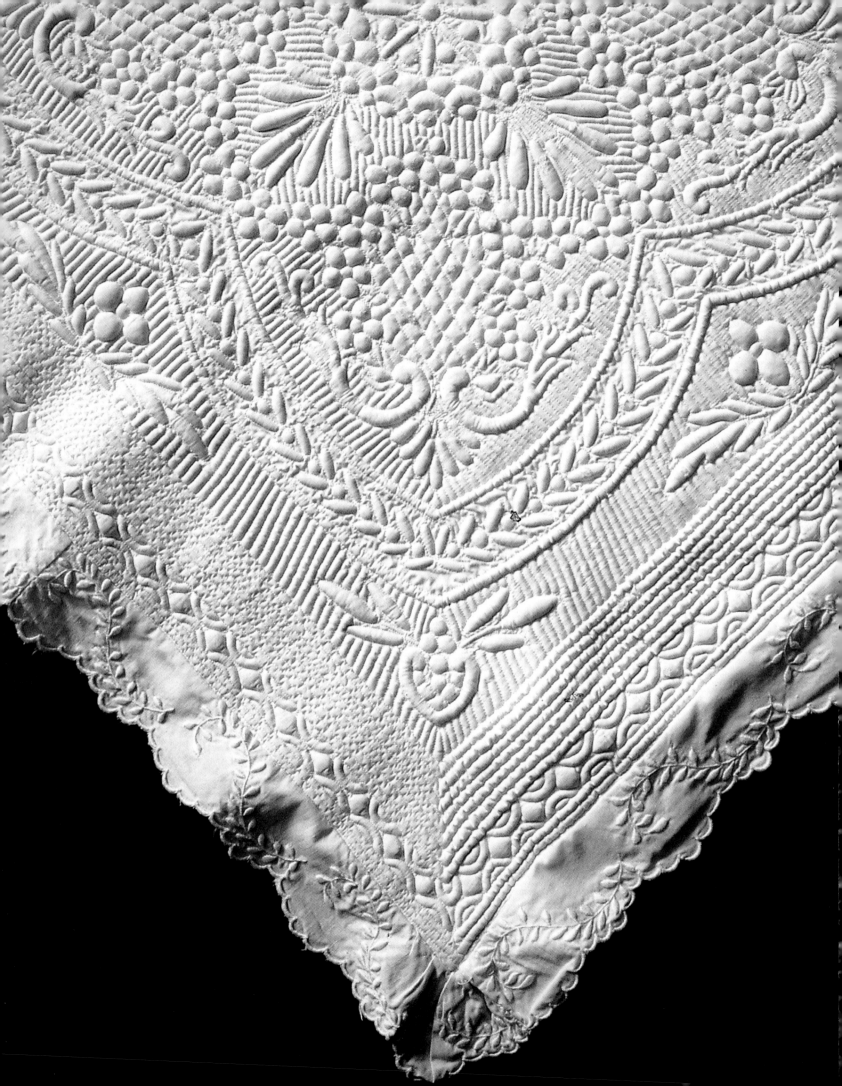

Raised embroidery – stitched works from group 2

In 1770, Saint Aubin, embroiderer to King Louis XVI, collected in this group the most beautiful raised embroideries[1] having the common trait on the inside: the "relief", but a relief much sought after in the purest expression of art. In this group are the 'piqûres de Marseille', 'broderie emboutie', 'broderie de Marseille', 'piqué de Marseille', and 'boutis' all raised in a method that differs slightly from one to the other… All require the qualities of patience, care and virtuosity, only truly acquired from much practice. During the Century of Light, professional embroiderers made Marseilles famous for its embroideries.

The mixing of the different types of embroidery leads to huge confusion, the result of not having precise information during that period. This confusion, which at the time profited international trade, provokes the downfall of our national textile heritage, to the detriment of a region, which knew glory, fame, and riches, thanks to these perfected stitching techniques.

Definitions

Several definitions have been given: the first, written by men and elaborated on by men, are not totally satisfactory. They are incomplete or lack precision. With a few well-chosen words the only man to have felt and spoken of the statistics that the 'boutis' does not have in common with the others, is Mistral. Paying special attention to his time, Mistral dedicates to this Decorative Art, in a few lines, the exact distinction of the 'boutis':

"Le boutis, ouvrage divin,
Qui ressemble à un pré dont le givre
Broda de blanc les feuilles et les pousses."

Frédéric Mistral
Calendal, Chant III

'The boutis, work divine,
Which resembles a meadow whose frost
Embroiders in white leaves and shoots.'

The interior embroideries, in relief, are created from a piece of cotton or silk, lined with cotton of a looser weave – never butter muslin as is used for Trapunto. Several imperfect definitions have tried to explain these raised embroideries, but the handful of information from several documents permits an elaboration on the different types.

For each type there are two principal characteristics that are the same:
– Two layers of fabric at the beginning, stretched on a frame
– Three stages to completion:
   1. The design
   2. The stitching
   3. The stuffing or the wadding.

"As soon as all the designs have been stitched, the frame is turned, then with a bodkin or the head of a large pin, more or less cotton thread is crammed between the two layers of fabric." (Saint Aubin, *L'art du Brodeur.*)

From the 17th to the 19th century, the raised embroideries were both successful and glorious (to this day, the last date known is on a 'vane', dated 1869).

Here are the differences between these different embroideries:

Piqûre de Marseille: the designs are fine, sylphlike, outlining the forms. They are outlined in running or backstitch. The tufts of wadding are introduced into the vermiculated channels with the help of a flexible stalk. Sometimes the stuffing was indigo or pink in order to increase the importance of the design.

Broderie emboutie: the motifs have slightly more volume. As soon as the relief is finished, the work is turned, and the ends are held in place with the help of a French knot.

Broderie de Marseille: having stuffed the large motifs, the spaces left are filled with embroidery stitches (satin stitch… French knots… sewing on pearls).

Piqué de Marseille: the raised motifs overlap one another. The fabric requires no care, but in order to prevent buckling, a few motifs are embroidered here and there without being stuffed.

Boutis: the whole surface is raised, or almost all. The motifs are not the biggest. The spaces between the motifs are filled with vermicelli (channels through which the tufts of cotton are passed) either in straight lines or in arcs.

A mixture of these last three categories plus the technique of wadding were sometimes used on the same piece of work. The application of all the above are found both on clothes and on pieces for the bed.

Preceding page:
Perfect balance of forms. The relief is particularly chiselled.

Embroidery and 'boutis' of Marseilles.   *Marseilles stitching.*

Marseilles stitching.

34

Marseilles 'picqûres'

The 'boutis'

In comparison with 'couvertures piquées' (wadded), real 'boutis' are known by their transparency. Placed against light, light passes through the fabric along the lines of stitches, which is not the case for wadded items, where the surface remains opaque.

The origin of the word 'boutis' could come from several sources, all interesting and complementing one another. For the people of the area, the word itself contains many meanings.

Around the 'boutis'… words…
" – boutiholo: bubble, sack
– boutihoula: to swell the skin
– boutis: hollow and downy when talking of boughs
– boutis: piqué de Marseille
– boufigo: bulb, bubble
– boufigeous: swollen
– embouti: stuffed, needle point."
The little treasure of Félibrige – Frédéric Mistral
In the *Quillet dictionary of the French Language*
– boutis: traces left by the boar and by its snout its search point.
– Bouter: to put, to push.
In the Provencal dictionary
– name of the needle which creates the hole through which the cotton stuffing is introduced. It has given its name to the place where the stuffing makes the relief.
In the supplement of *Vesti Prouvençau*, Simone and Estelle Nougier quote J. Bourilly:

"**Boutis**: type of stitched embroidery. The fabric that was to be stitched was folded in two and had the design drawn on and followed in double lines by hand stitching. In between the stitches a tuft of twisted cotton was introduced around a flexible metal bodkin (tool that called a 'boutis'). This was cotton tuft also formed, between the stitches, folds that drew out the design."

Le trésor du Félibrige, (p.352) says:
"Piqué de Marseille, needlepoint on white fabric that the girls of Cassis and La Ciotat embroidered in the past."

"D'autro, pougnent la telo fino
Fan lou boutis" *Calendou*, F. Mistral.

The expression 'au boutis' used in the inventory of Madame Conil in 1758, in Arles, was not always used in the current language of the day. The 'boutis' were rare and reserved for the elite, the more fortunate. On the same train of thought, 'au lacet' is found. From 1765, the English blockade was to encircle Marseilles in a noose, preventing commercial trade. Many manufacturers closed. The women continued to practise the techniques for their domestic needs, either at home or in little workshops. In the countryside around Nimes, the word 'boutis'

was not used. Every inventory that was consulted – from 1650 onwards – every human resource that was asked, over 90 years of age, who knew the shape of these needles specific to the 'boutis', who owned 'vanes' and 'jupons' hardly ever or never mentioned this expression. It was used more in the Marseilles region, as well as in Provence. On the other hand, they are quoted as 'piqûres de Marseille' in the inventory of Charles de Baschi and 'piqué' in all the inventories shown.

The base of a rich bridal 'jupon', embroidered in 'boutis' to a height of approximately 50 cm.

White, the colour of the divine, the symbol of purity.

The beautiful history of the 'boutis'.

The wedding wardrobes from the Nimes region conceal more priceless treasures made in 'boutis'. Presents offered at the wedding, preciously kept, and in perfect condition, brightly illustrating the unions between the men and women of the previous century. Thanks to the loving care of their owners, the whiteness of the immaculate fabric has not been submitted to the ravages of time. The stories which give life back to these 'vanes' and 'jupons' from times long ago bring to light every day new questions that, until now, have not been answered.

Mme R… is 95 years of age and lives in Beauvoisin. In her childhood, Beauvoisin had only nine hearths, that is to say about forty inhabitants. In the family 'mas' surrounded by her treasures, she spoke of her great aunts Mira and Julie, who made 'boutis'. She spoke especially about Mira who married in 1870. She made 'vanes' and 'couvertons', all sorts of masterpieces which have happily illustrated the pages of this book.

Jeanne M… lives in Aimarques. She is 79 years old. She speaks tenderly of her grandmother Albertine who lived in Blauzac, near Uzès. Albertine was born in 1845 and the masterpieces that she created are intact, perfectly conserved by the hands of her descendants.

Mira and Albertine made their 'boutis' at the opposite ends of the Gard, one at the gateway of the Cévennes, the other not far from the Vaunage, the rich plain not far from the sea. They were both born "in the middle of the century".

One was protestant, the other catholic…

NOTES

1. Broderie en rondes-bosses, broderie en bosses, broderie enlevée or eslevée, broderie emboutie, broderie haute: expressions used to qualify raised embroidery. (Saint Aubin pp10, 11, 22, 36; Farcy pp17, 27; Dillmont p.186). See bibliography.

2. From about AD 395 to 1453.

3. Name given to eight expeditions undertaken from the 11th to 13th Centuries by Christian Europe against the Muslim East.

4. This date is indicated on a map illustrating the progression of printed calico in Europe at the museum of fabric printing – Mulhouse.

5. Date given in the exhibition catalogue of 1988: Façon Arlésienne – Musée Arlaten, Arles.

6. Manufacturers who made everything that touched the garniture of the bed (the counterpane, the 'vane' and the cover).

7. Padded or stitched cloth, 50 cm square; people used to have it under the baby's bottom to protect their clothes.

8. Fabric made with and cotton, both in the warp and the weft. *Dictionnaire universel de commerce* by Jacques Savary des Bruslons.

9. Printed flowers in the style of fabrics imported from Turkey.

10. Anecdote cited in 'Les Arts Décoratifs en Provence' by M.J. Baumelle, Edisud.

11. Gênes and Cadix were the two trading posts for the exportation and importation of goods. Cadix dealt with the commercial exchanges in the Indian Ocean.

12. I gardened, I cultivated "four vegetables" and attached very little importance to it.

A real 'boutis' is known by its transparency, whereas wadding lets no light through.

38

From marriage to birth :

the boutis in the trousseau

The House of Baschi

The yellowed pages of precious books have marriage contracts and inventories sleeping between their pages that teem with knowledge concerning previous times during which stitching techniques were being practised. The royal or imperial[1] lawyers give in their fine writing, dampened with black ink, detailed and precise accounts of estates according to their social status. The archives of each county also allow us to picture the framework of family life.

Not very far from Nimes in the Gard, we are going to gently climb the monumental stairs and enter the chateau of the Marquis d'Aubais via the grand entrance. It is a small Versailles, in the image of that of the Sun King's, Louis XIV. Louis de Baschi started construction, but could not complete it, as in 1685 he had to take refuge in Geneva due to the revocation of the Edict of Nantes[2].

At this time, many Huguenots were forced to leave the country for fear of having to renounce their religion. Louis de Baschi died in exile. With calm reinstated, his son Charles was to continue his work and complete the construction of the castle.

Thirty-four bedrooms awaited us! It was a real treasure trove to be able to open the doors of the armoires and the wardrobes, to rummage in the corners. The library, with its sixteen thousands books, the portrait gallery, many wall-hangings, sophisticated ornaments and its walnut furniture proved the opulence and the erudition of the Marquis and depicted the style of the period.

Luxurious fabrics covered the walls, chairs and beds. The off-cuts of striped silk, satin, chiffon, printed calico and cotton adorned furniture and beds. Stitched 'couvertures' had their place in every bedroom whether they were printed calicos of a white 'basin' or of a single colour, but also of silk. They covered beds everywhere with elegance and brightness. This refinement was even to be found in the cook's bedroom and that of the chaplain! By Jove, M. de Baschi knew how to look after his household!

But it is in the main room, found at the bottom of the grand staircase, and not the display bedroom where we were to find the most beautiful treasures: two 'courtepointes' in 'piqûres de Marseille'.

In this way, Diane de Rozel, his wife, who liked blue and green, was able to appreciate these 'courtepointes' of raised embroidery, orders that were probably made in the workshops of Marseilles or Nîmes in the 17th or 18th centuries. So it was possible to live in the country and possess the furniture[3] of kings. The 'broderies embouties' were luxury pieces, rare and also proved the excellent taste of the country nobles. Right in the middle of the prohibition, eight printed calico 'couvertures' are mentioned, two are particularly worn, confirming their usage in that century.

Portrait of Charles de Baschi.

The Baschi family was originally from Italy. Its name belonged to one of the noblest families of Florence in 1215. They came to Provence around 1413. In 1478, Guichard de Baschi was attached to Louis d'Anjou, King of Naples and Count of Provence.

Charles de Baschi, Marquis d'Aubais, Baron du Cailar was born in 1686. He studied at schools in Toulouse and Clermont and at the Duga Academy, which he left at 18 to become a Musketeer. He fought in the campaign of 1705, and was decommissioned. Very erudite, he divided his life between Aubais and Paris. He married Diane de Rozel at Castres in 1708, and died in 1777. His daughter married the Count d'Urre from Carpentras.

The castle at Aubais of Charles de Baschi.

In the bedroom of Monsieur the Marquis.

– A blue, white and black wall hanging, covering the whole room, except for above the doors.
– A walnut bed, with three mattresses, a feather bed and its bolster, 2 'couvertures' in white flannelette and a stitched printed calico 'courtepointe'.

In the apartment of Madame, the first bedroom.

– Two sofas in walnut, one covered in yellow serge with a little yellow serge mattress, the other with no mattress, yellow seat and back and edgings of striped white satin.
– A walnut armchair with floral seat and back, and green damask edging.
– Five chairs with ornate backs of green and white 'bourrette'.
– One chair with a white striped satin back.
– A walnut bed with a straw mattress, two mattresses, and a feather bed with its bolster, a pillow, another cover of printed and stitched red and white floral calico, a bed cover made of several cherry-red velvet fabrics, and three bed bases the same. The curtains were of green serge and a 'coussinière' of chiffon.

In the little bedroom at the end of the first bedroom, on the right-hand side on entering.

– A walnut bed with a straw mattress, a mattress, a feather bed and its bolster, a 'couverture' of white flannelette, another of a white fabric and another of stitched yellow satin, and a bed cover of green serge with yellow braid and ribbons, with its bed bases of the same fabric.
– Two chairs with ornate backs of green and white 'bourrette'

In another little bedroom next to the other.

– A slatted bed with a straw mattress, a mattress bolster, 2 sheets, a woollen 'couverture', and a little white 'couvre-pieds'.

In a bedroom.

– The Duchess' bed, held together by two iron triangles. The cover is made up of different bands of coloured satin, with yellow 'filoselle' fabric curtains.
– A blue silk 'courtepointe' and its three bed bases.
– A 'courtepointe' of stitched white 'basin'.
– Worn flannelette 'couverture'.
– Two walnut chairs covered in blazing green and white stripes of 'bourrette'.

In a little dim bedroom, next to the last one.

– A bed with a straw mattress, a mattress, 2 sheets and a woollen 'couverture', a 'courtepointe' of white 'basin', and a bolster.

In the castle chaplain's bedroom, next to the bedroom of Madame, Countess of Urre.

– A walnut bed with a straw mattress, a mattress, a feather bed and a bolster, 2 sheets, a white stitched 'couverture', and another of red floral printed calico on the topside with borders of white fabric, also stitched, and a bed cover in crimson serge with white braid and ribbons.

In the main room, at the bottom of the grand staircase.

– A wall hanging of 11 pieces, 9 that are 9' high and 2 that are 9,5' high, representing the story of Toby.

In the storehouses.

– Thirty-four wall hangings of different sizes, depicting people and countryside.
– Two trunks, one on top of the other, with their locks and keys, containing:
  Number 1: A piece of blue damask, with yellow braiding, destined for a bed; six embroidered armchair coverings, wool and silk on canvas; fourteen matching chair coverings.
  Number 2: Thirty-four pieces of embroidered canvas, wool and silk, two with the coat-of-arms of the deceased Monsieur le Marquis d'Aubais, and thirty-two others for beds, chairs and footstools.
– An armoire in pale wood, without shelves, with its lock and key, containing: Six 'couvertures', two of white fabric and stitched, one of red printed calico and stitched, one of stitched green silk and two in white flannelette, with a little 'piqûre de Marseille'
– Three other pale wood armoires, containing: two 'courtepointes' in 'piqûre de Marseille'.

In the housekeeper's bedroom.

– A walnut bed with two mattresses, a straw mattress, a feather bed and a bolster, sheets, a woollen 'couverture', another of stitched printed calico and a valence made from sheets of white fabric.

In a bedroom.

– A walnut bed with two mattresses, a feather bed and its bolster, two sheets, a blue and white stitched printed calico 'couverture', and another, also stitched, of several pieces of fabric of different colours

In another bedroom next to the chapel.

– A walnut bed with two mattresses, a feather bed and a bolster, sheets, a stitched white 'couverture', a stitched cover made of pink silk, and red and white printed calico curtains.

In the cook's bedroom.

– A small folding bed with little mattresses and a little feather bed with its bolster, sheets, a woollen 'couverture', stitched 'couvertures' – one red and the other one grey.

In the first bedroom, above the library, on the left.

– A walnut bed with two mattresses, a feather bed and a bolster, a woollen 'couverture' and another of a white stitched fabric, a valence of white calico printed with red flowers and the sky, and a back of different coloured fabrics.

In the butler's bedroom.

– A walnut field bed with a straw mattress, a mattress, a feather bed and a bolster, two sheets and a printed calico 'couverture' with old stitching.

In the display bedroom.

– A walnut bed with three mattresses, a feather bed and a bolster, a 'couverture' of stitched printed calico, the cover, a 'courtepointe' and bed bases of red damask, and the thick curtain of red linen.

Of the thirty stitched 'couvertures', five of them are silk; one of them is noticeable by its description: it is a stitched silk cover, an extremely rare piece for that period. Other 'couvertes'[4] of flannelette complete this 1777 inventory. Thirty is an impressive number for 'courtepointes' made with these stitching techniques. In the castle, all social levels were catered for: nobles and servants adorned their beds with beautiful and comfortable 'vanes'[5] pleasing to touch, and pleasing to the eye, highly appreciated for the standard produced and for the new fabric, sometimes by block printing.

The Marquis' coat-of-arms appears on the chair tapestries, and probably decorates the 'courtepointes' in 'piqûre de Marseille'. On important masterpieces it was normal to include the blazon or seal signifying its belonging to that house[6]. In fact, the tapestry-maker could embroider these at the last minute by carefully handling the space in the central medallion or in the corners.

The Baschi family[7], originally from Italy, were nobles from 1215. They were one of the richest families in Florence, as was the Medici family. Attached to the King of Naples, Louis d'Anjou from 1381, they moved to Provence around 1413. Unfortunately, due to the 'mistral' and lack of wits, neither the precious 'chauffoirs'[8] used to temper the large chimneys with their flamboyant piles of wood nor the comfortable dressing gowns with 'broderie emboutie', nor the delicate bed bonnets adorned with a leafy pattern for sleeping in the hollows of the Duchess' feather beds can be found in the inventories.

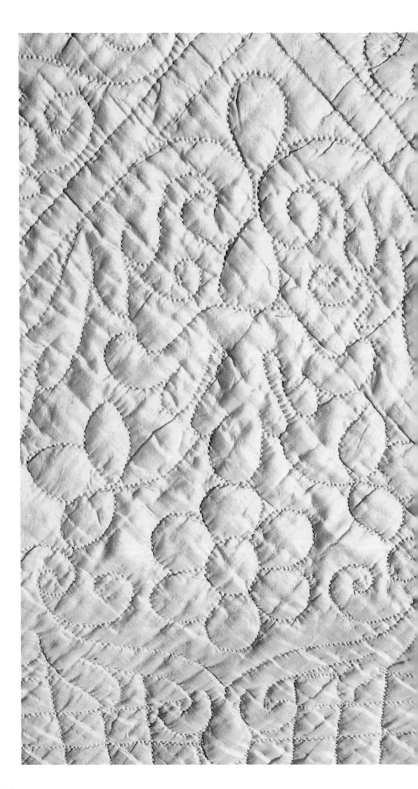

In the first bedroom, at the end on the right hand side as you enter; there is a 'courtepointe' of yellow satin.

In the shadow of castles

After the Revolution in 1789, the bourgeois of the business world and the landowners represented the rising classes. Philosophers such as Jean-Jacques Rousseau, Voltaire and Diderot were to lead a current of thought which was to cultivate the relationships between citizens. Man was to be at the centre of everyone's thoughts. The countrymen and the agricultural workers would try to acquire, with more or less success, a little more freedom. They were to have to wait another century before the improved standard of living was visible on the ground, as shown by the inventories.

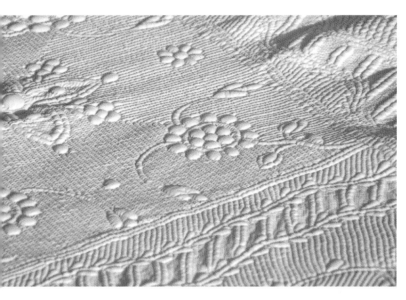

The 'boutis' have found their place in the farmhouses and country houses.
The most modest were made in household fabric,
embroidered by the light of the 'caléous' in the peasant houses.

Copy of 4 inventories showing the evolution of the trousseau during the 19th century.

1. Here is a marriage contract from the beginning of the century between Madeleine de Clarensac and David de Saint Côme by the lawyer Mazoyer:
Regime dotal: 100F and 1 cabinet in walnut (armoire)
1 silver chatelaine (clip with silver chains)
1 Holy Spirit in gold
3 shrouds (sheets)
3 tablecloths
2 napkins
200F in vines on 1400m²

2. Example of a more precise trousseau in which the bride appears to have a little more freedom. Marriage of 11th March 1820, recorded by Me Auquier of Calvisson, between M. Émile Maroyer, farmer, and Mlle Cécile Jullian:
5 linen sheets with scalloped edges
8 tablecloths
1 white stitched 'vanne' (boutis)
1 embroidered mantelpiece cloth
kitchen objects
1 diamond of the Jeannette cut (a Provencal cut)
1 medallion plus its chain, in gold
1 butterfly in diamonds
1 gold ring
1 silver chatelaine
1 pair of earrings

3. 1807, 6th February: M. Farel Pierre and Marie Jaulnes of Congénies:
6 bed sheets
6 tablecloths
6 bath towels
6 hand towels
1 silver chatelaine (often a present from the bridegroom to the bride)
1 gold ring
1 walnut stool

4. In 1859, in front of Me Peyre, lawyer at Calvisson: Marriage between Jacques Fournier from Saint Cômes and Adeline Maumejan:
9 bed sheets
9 tablecloths
9 napkins
9 hand towels

These trousseau show progressive enrichment: from 3 sheets, tablecloths, towels and sometimes hand towels, moving rapidly to 6, and then to 9.

Prosperity was found in the large towns where commerce could develop, on the rich plains in wine growing or arable areas sharing a fertile soil, along the length of water courses where gardens and orchards were plentiful (irrigation was a luxury), in the ports where commercial exchanges took place with great intensity. Don't say that at this time Marseilles was France's third port! In the lower Alps and the Cévennes, the 'gavots'[9] came down from the mountains and moved into the farms for the season in order to earn a few pennies. The 'boutis' had its place in these surroundings, in the 'mas'[10] in the countryside, in imposing 'bastides',[11] at houses where people had a little wealth, and especially at those houses where there was a well, as that is a precious asset in the Midi. On its own, it was a sign of real wealth as both watering the garden and domestic activities flow from it.

The inside of the country house belonging to the family of Mira, Lyse and Julie…

Albertine embroiders her trousseau

At the beginning of the 19th century, Albertine prepared her trousseau. As a little girl, she learnt from the hands of her mother to master the cross-stitch used to mark the household linen. Around the age of 8, she completed a magnificent sampler, signed with both her first and last name. It was her first major piece of work. The apprenticeship of 'savoir-faire' started at home. Albertine was yet to master all the embroidery stitches in order to personalise and decorate the finer sheets, caps and headscarves, shirts and swishing 'jupons'.

In the village square in the shade of the plane trees, under the fig trees in the garden or even in the early evening, in the company of the girls of her own age, she embroidered adornments for the bridal bed and the dream 'jupons'. On the linen, hemp or cotton canvas, Albertine wrote with her needle with help from the relief of the threads, her hopes, sewn in letters and love arabesques. From the making of clothes to the upkeep of linen, she learnt these indispensable details for the good upkeep of a house. The village dressmaker would put

the finishing touches to her knowledge, but would not deliver the secrets of the cut; for the last part of her apprenticeship, she needed to go into town.

Having mastered all this 'savoir-faire', Albertine could at last 'boutis' her marriage 'jupon'. But who taught her to do this specific form of needlework?

The answer is probably found in her nearby area, near the people that she mixed with… but it is still surrounded in mystery.

Napoleon III travelling kit.

45

Manon gets married

Manon was all excited: she was getting married to a young man from the neighbouring village. The families knew each other, and were happy. Between people of the same standing, business went fairly well. The marriage contract would be signed at the village solicitor. In the wedding basket, the bride had put her beautiful white linen trousseau, the gilded objects[12] she had amassed during the past few months thanks to her personal work, money and her precious marriage armoire in sculpted walnut. The promise from his side brought land, the house and all forms of bricks and mortar, as inheritance followed the male line.

For this exceptional and happy event, all the rooms in the farmhouse had been polished; everything shined. The horses were dressed up and the entrance porch was decorated with thick garlands of box, dotted with flowers. The countryside was in harmony with the sentiments of the day. When the ceremony took place in Spring, the air would adorn itself with the scents of flowers, thyme and rosemary. In the hills, the rock rose bushes and the golden broom flash thousands of sparkles. Near the mazets[13] the scent of the lilac hangs heavy in the air and the irises mark the grass on the bank with blue. Others prefer Autumn, as in this season the light is gentler and comes to lightly caress the open country and slopes during the meal,

after the intense activity of the grape harvest. The harvest in, there is time to see and marry off the children.

The guests have come a long way, on charabancs, horses or on foot, across the garrigue[14], wearing their suits, 'jupons', with light, transparent lace lining their wicker baskets. The 'cotillons' of printed calico flying at the sound of the country flutes and the tambourines, twirling in the frenzied farandoles. In the outbuildings[15] whitened with lime mortar or in the courtyard in the shade of the nettle tree, the meals were never-ending, punctuated by songs and compliments in the language of Mistral[16] and the 'galéjades'[17] delighting the audience. The youth of the surrounding area would celebrate, the girls perhaps meeting their future husbands and dancing with them to the point of exhaustion, their heads spinning.

The fiancé offered a silver chatelaine and the beater. The irons were often engraved. As to the heater, it would keep her feet warm…

A bridal 'jupon' monogrammed with the initials L.P. The young girl offered her fiancé a "love token", a bracelet plaited from her own hair.

For this unique, long awaited day, Manon had embroidered a long time ago her 'jupon' in 'boutis'. She knew what she wanted: the effect of movement at the base, with the light borders swaying in the wind, the boughs bending under bunches of flowers, and the vases of hearts overflowing with love. Having hesitated between printed calico and brightly coloured silks, she chose green, the colour of hope and silk, for its lightness and sober elegance. Her slender size would be accentuated perfectly and the pleats gave the 'jupon' its volume, the camisole perfectly cut, exploiting her assets. Manon is beautiful, and she knows it, and wants to please her betrothed; a flirt, she graciously lifts up the base of her wedding dress in order that the whole congregation could admire the beauty of her work and would not doubt her ability to run the household effectively. She received from the hand of her betrothed the silver chatelaine[18] which she fixed to her slight build, as well as a magnificent beater engraved with traditional symbols.

A wedding costume

The bridal 'jupon' in 'basin' or lawn, created in 'boutis' as white as snow, is an underskirt[19] as they like to remember the keepers of the "vesti provençau". It became part of the wedding costume, but it can be worn under a silk or coloured printed calico dress. The bride would lift up her dress in a pretty movement, and secure it with a dart, falling like a drape, letting the 'broderie emboutie' be seen. In this way, the decoration – embroidered more, or less - could be admired, and the competence of the young bride witnessed. The 'jupon', as an everyday garment, was for working. In bygone days in the village, the character, the ways of making it and the tastes of each girl were known and were whispered from ear to ear. In the winter evenings, during the 'castagnade'[20], or during the long summer evenings, in the cool, their tongues went at nineteen to the dozen. The boys imparted what they knew, and also what they thought they knew, and with a knowing look, spoke highly of the opportunities of the future, of getting married, already envious of those who had had the chance to slip a ring on the finger of one of the pearls of the region. The expression "Celle-là, oui, elle est capable!"[21] (That one, oh yes, she's a good choice!) accompanied by a thumbs up, is still a saying in the Midi.

It is unusual to find in the inventories a trace of the 'jupon' with its 'boutis', whereas the stitched 'cotillons' and the wadded 'jupons' are clearly marked. The handing down was done though the hands of women. With seriousness, as with the keepers of the Greek temples in ancient times, they left the marriage treasures to be passed on from one generation to the next, from mother to daughter. They reproduced or reinvented the works that have travelled through thousands of years. In offering to others the most precious things they wore, they continued the memory of a tradition, the imprint of their southern French civilisation.

A beautiful fullness, of two to three metres in length around the base, and sometimes more, with an average height of between 80 to 90 cm, these 'jupons' have two parts of unequal importance, separated most of the time by a border which defines the two creative techniques: wadding and 'boutis'. When the majority was given over to the wadded part, it was for economic or other reasons, the section of 'boutis' shrank or disappeared. Several styles were to share the glory of a single day. Modest 'jupons' where the white colour compensates for the lack of embellishment was moving in its simplicity. The filling of the lozenges with the help of cotton 'bourre',[22] in relief either from the wadding technique or that of the 'piqué-bourré' or even that of the 'boutis'.

The finery of a queen…

Bridal 'jupons'

The 'jupon' with its garden maze, or flowering vases or baskets, flowers cut without their stalks, share the space at the bottom, presenting an apparent disorder. Looking properly gives the pleasure of discovering hearts and signs of love, finely stitched with emotion, showing the intimate nature of the promise. Thanks to these precious indicators you catch yourself wanting to find their Christian name. The imagination sketches a delicate portrait, outlining a silhouette in the mist, a fleeting presence.

The 'jupon-frises', named as such for better understanding, already show a more studied organisation. Successive light and elegant borders of branches and floral explosions in heart vases undulate more than the original model. Everything about them breathes grace, beauty and rays of love.

But the most elaborately decorated one, without contest, is that of the garden 'jupon', as their composition is evident and carefully thought over. Springing from repeating vases or baskets of a pleasant height (50 or 54 cm), it is similar to that of the garden 'jupon' of printed brushed calico[23] that was the fashion under Louis XV. It makes one think that there is some kind of bond between the two, visible in the conception of the branches that climb across it. The baskets or the heart-baskets symbolise the anchorage in life, anchorage in the family, the principal that lies at the base of the Indian tree of life.

The area worked in 'boutis' varies in height on each stuffed white cotton bridal 'jupon'. The fabric, richness and composition of the motifs used could indicate the social standing, the identity of the region, or even a village. The compassion of the creator, the unconscious or conscious traditional inspirations, and sensitive qualities give sense and emotion to these textile labyrinths. The conjunction of all these elements constitutes the essence of the art.

The wedding dress. The 'jupon' embroidered in 'boutis' was worn underneath the dress (this one was photographed at the Musée des traditions Populaires in Draguignan).

Bridal 'jupon':
the undulating borders create
the dancing movement.

The grace of a branch, which bends
under the whiteness of the fabric.

Other wedding presents

The 'vane'[24] is a square 'courtepointe' measuring 1.5m each side, and in fact does not cover the bed entirely. It is obvious, once the length of time it takes to make a 'vane' in 'boutis' is understood, that a young girl preparing and embroidering her trousseau could not possess a great deal, unless she belonged to a well-off family who could order it from a workshop. Disregarding other domestic duties, we could calculate approximately a year of her life being spent on this piece alone.

From the beginning of the 19th century, a number of stitched 'courtepointe' either of printed calico or silk appeared in the inventories of artisans and 'bastidans',[25] but there is no trace of the 'boutis'. Several hypotheses might explain the causes. The word 'boutis' was not widely used and that of 'piqué' was in popular use and was incorrectly applied to many works, having confused the techniques.

The expressions "couverture piquée blanche de basin"[26] and "courtepointe piquée d'indienne"[27] appear to better define the different types. On the other hand, the higher price of the former, the precision on the white and on the fabric – the 'basin' being the cotton – could have constituted a serious approach to the 'boutis', but it is certainly the evidence on the ground that will permit us to lift a corner of the veil.

Mme Pontier, whose family is originally from Blauzac in the Gard, tells, "The 'vane' in 'boutis' was one of the wedding pre-sents. Accompanied by a knitted 'couverture', the wedding bed was embellished, even in August! At the same time in those days, the cover for the cradle matching the 'vane' was also given, clearly expressing a justifiable desire for children".

The size of the 'vane' did not permit the whole bed to be covered, and was sometimes accompanied by assorted 'coussinières'[28]. In this way the nuptial bed was adorned with marital wishes, cornucopias, fruits and flowers, branches swathed in foliage, tender hearts and pairs of birds cooing their love to each other, all of which could only foretell favourable auspices for the future.

The 'vane' was passed from woman to woman in the same family. With the same degree of care as is given to love letters and precious shawls, it was kept out of sight, in walnut armoires. It represented the modesty of women, their secret garden. Albertine offered hers to Marie, her daughter-in-law, who in turn gave it to Jeanne, her daughter, who gave it to Suzanne, her daughter, who gave it to Beatrice as a present…

The 'vane' is the masterpiece of a mature woman who possesses a known 'savoir-faire'. The composition comes from a visible maturity of mind: the harmony of the forms and the pronounced relief of the motifs have the status of a technique experimented in and mastered.

*The washerwoman's beater is decorated with a **coin** and a Maltese cross. Museon Arlaten, Arles, negative belonging to J.L. Mabit, B. Delgado.*

Marriage 'vane' from the Napoleonic period.

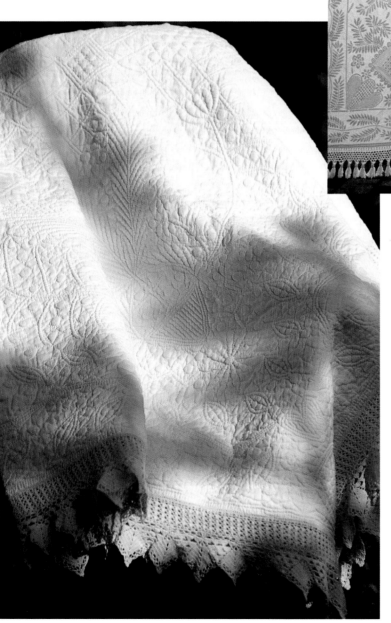

Marriage 'courtepointe' belonging to Louche Adélaïde, born in 1829 at Marsillargues.

The hands of women

For birth, it was normal to make 'pétassons'. This activity involved many generations of women living under the same roof. The word 'pétasson' comes from 'pétas' (you must pronounce the 's'), a scrap of fabric which is used to repair sheets or clothes. In its current usage, 'pétas' means both scrap and fabric. On the other side of the Rhone, in Provence, the same object became the 'pétassoun', and everywhere in the Midi, it is called a 'piqué' because of the way it is made, 'bourrasse' or 'bourrasson' from the cotton 'bourre' that was placed in the interior, 'couverton' from its use, and 'culachon' and 'vanon'. The vocabulary is rich and visual for the designing of these padded pieces of different sizes.

Often only made to measure depending on what was needed in white cotton fabrics were 'rouenneries' or small motif printed calicos. They were very absorbent, and protected the clothes of the persons who had the child on their knee. Nappies appeared around 1955, and washing machines were widespread around 1965, but until then, the maintenance of linen by hand washing was hard work. At the wash place, the baby's linens were washed separately, before those of the adults. The 'bugadière' soaped it beside the water, and it was left to the Marseilles soap to render the linen whiter than white.

To go to the wash place, the women chose the best day of the week, when the water was at its clearest in the large basin, because it had been cleaned the night before, or better still, early in the morning as they wanted to profit from the still, clear water.

In soaping the little baby vests, bibs and bonnets, they would tell in great detail the life of their 'petitou' (little one), its progress, smiles and events, and from the content of the conversation, the child took an important place in society, outside of the family circle. In light of this behaviour, we can better understand the desire to mark the arrival of the newborn into this world with exceptional, tangible, visible and traditional presents, called 'boutis'.

The 'caluchon' or 'piqué'

Presents for the new mother

Salt, eggs, bread and a matchstick, accompanied by the vows of the newborn:

Que voste enfant siegue:
That your child be:

San coume la sau
As healthy as salt

Poulit coume un iou
As pretty as an egg

Bon coume lou pan
As good as the bread

Dre coume uno brouqueto
As straight as a match.

The 'péquélets' linen was always washed separately, the first time in pure water.

52

Little princes

With muffled footsteps, we enter into the world of the young child, one which is blessed with innocence, magical moments that are always too short, smiles, lullabies and soft words, making up the language of happiness. Moments of grace, light caresses, the little hand that holds onto your finger… these pictures are etched forever in a woman's mind. Embroidered from the interior with infinite patience, these 'boutis', made with love, adorned with flowers and other symbols as if to attract the benevolence of the gods, are destined for little angels. Granny, mother and godmother created little jewels with their needles so that the precious moments were even more precious. With fingers as light as fairies, in the evening gatherings, the women produced translucent works, giving a full measure of a love that knows no bounds. The beautiful and the white - colour of the divine, were to confer on the religious ceremony of the baptism, and the traditional customs linked to the birth, all the solemnity and grace they were due.

Each area of France has its own peculiarities, and the Occitan region is no exception. Whether they are from Marseilles, Nîmes or Draguignan, these works of art reserved for childhood and made in 'boutis' have however certain differences. In the collection studied, the shape is more often rectangular than not; perfect squares are not found, no doubt because of deformations in the fabric, in the warp or weft, or from the quantity of stuffing used or from the way the fabric was cut. Provence borders hers with smooth festoons, the Languedoc, more soberly with straight lines. The ornamental functions and compositions were in even numbers. To make an appearance at a special occasion (baptisms and journeys), the 'going out boutis', decorated more than any other, was adorned with lace.

On these light sculptures, it was pleasing to follow the curving leaves with the eye, admiring the raised quality of the flowers and wreathes. The oak leaf and the daisy argue over their importance; acorns, stars, little bunches of grapes and swanlike birds were all part of the classical collection on these pieces.

The 'Musée Arlaten'[29] has amongst its many treasures a window dedicated to the bedroom. There, childrens' undergarments in 'broderie emboutie' can be discovered, made in Indian chiffon or fine lawn. These rare and precious documents from the 17th century let us appreciate at a glance the refinement of the aristocracy of the time, three centuries ago, and to give us knowledge of the oldest techniques: 'piqûre de Marseille' and 'broderie emboutie'.

The family of Mme Privat, the wife of the King's governor, at Beaucaire, depicted in the painting by Antoine Raspal around 1775-1780, breathes happiness. The baby with its pink cheeks is wearing a 'cache-maillot' matching the vest,

both of which were made in 'boutis'. They were adopted and reproduced in our campaigns with the same relief of little lozenges, after the Revolution. The testimony of a person, originally from Blauzac near Uzès, has confirmed this. The 'cache-maillot', the 'cache-brassière' and the cradle surround were all 'boutis' of this fashion.

In this way, 'vanons' with the initials of the child and the date of birth on top of the dream cradle watched over the sleep of other little princes.

At the end of the 19th century, the mechanical stitching of cotton replaced the precious 'boutis', but the Languedoc and Provence have always kept their taste for raised sections on our regional furniture and pottery.

NOTES

1. Officiating lawyers during the reign of a king or an emperor.
2. Signed in Nantes, in 1598, by Henri IV, the Edict of Nantes gave civil status to the Protestants (giving them freedom of thought, access to all posts and jobs) – ref no 2084, 23 March 1985.
3. Word used to design not only the furniture, but also the household linen.
4. Means 'couverture'.
5. A 'courtepointe' which did not cover the whole bed.
6. Signifying a noble, princely or royal family.
7. Research and inventories on the Baschi family were done by Mathias Baron-Martel.
8. Small pieces done in vermicelli that were either heated up or were used for warming. History states that these 'chauffoirs' were placed against the belly of women during birth.
9. These are the workers who came down from the mountains to help with the seasonal work (crop harvest, grape harvest, olive harvest).
10. Farms in the Midi.
11. Large low buildings surrounded by vines.
12. Gold jewellery (long chain, chain, cross, rings, pendants).
13. Stone cottage in the garrigue or in the vines. See note below.
14. Hills covered in vegetation that is specific to the Mediterranean region. Similar to scrub or brush land.
15. Buildings used to house the agricultural objects.
16. Frédéric Mistral was a felibre - a Provencal poet - and ardent defender of the Provencal traditions and the language.
17. Tall or funny stories.
18. The silver or metal chatelaine was made up of a double chain with a hook. The young bride hung her keys and her embroidery scissors from it.
19. See Le Vesti provençau.
20. Evenings when the chestnuts were cooked in a perforated pot placed on a tripod in the chimney.
21. In provencal, "aco oï! Es une affaïre"
22. Rough "woolly" cotton, not spun.
23. The 'pinceauteuses' managed to paint the printed motifs. It was precision work that was created with a paintbrush.
24. "De vano" in provençal, meaning 'courtepointe'.
25. Owners of the 'bastides'.
26. 'couverture' stitched in white 'basin'.
27. 'courtepointe' stitched on printed calico.
28. These were the covers, or pillow cases which hid the cushion.
29. Musée Arlaten is in Arles and was created by Frédéric Mistral.

The newborn baby's vest, made from muslin and cotton worked in 'boutis', padded with white cotton. Musée Arlaten, Arles, negative belonging to J.L.Mabit, B. Delgado.

Madame Privat and her daughters, by Antoine Raspal. Oil on canvas, 1775 – 1780. Musée Arlaten, Arles, plate belonging to J.L. Mabit, B. Delgado.

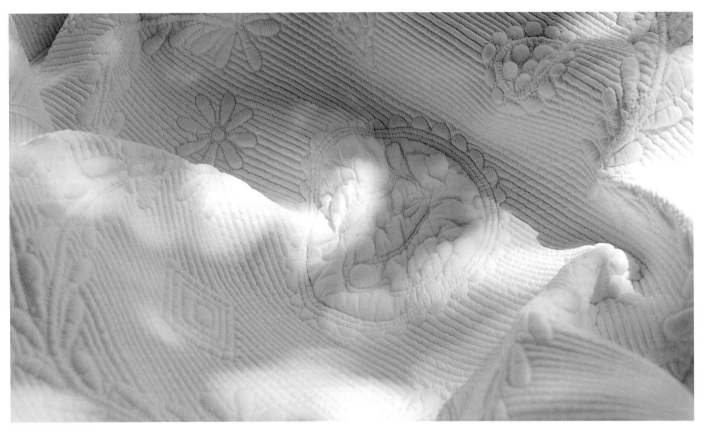

'Vanons' are little ceremonial 'vanes' that were placed on the bed of the newborn.

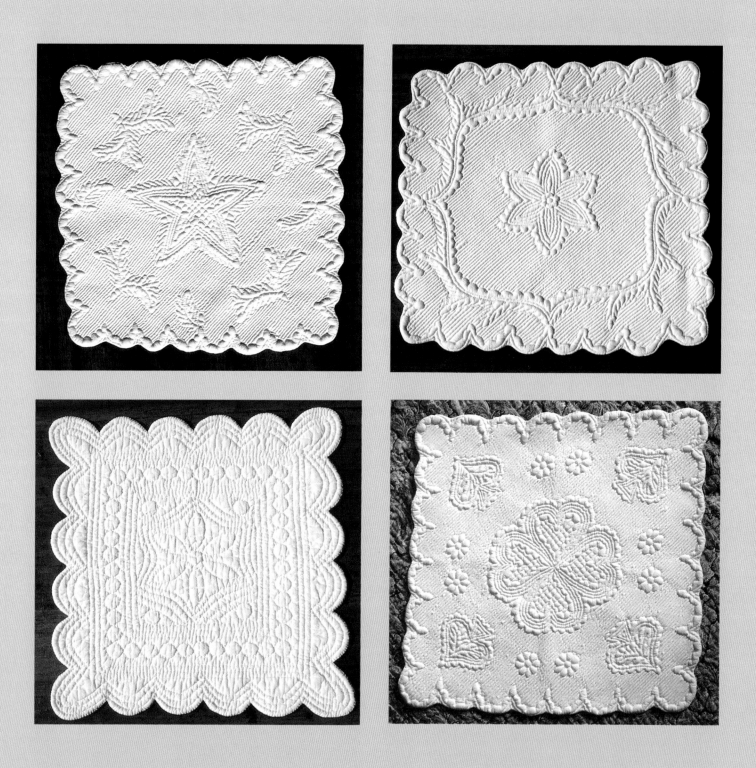

For the birth, the use was to make 'pétassons' or 'culachons'. According to Madame Amphoux, de Bernis,
"the child was presented along with the 'pétasson'…"

Pillowcases were called 'coussinières'.

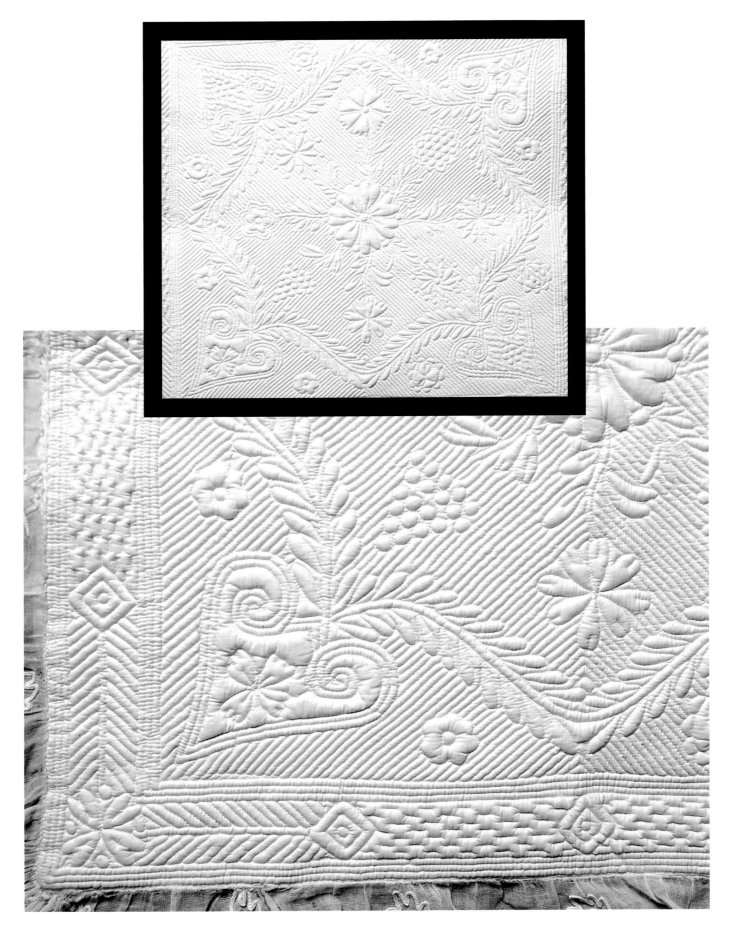

Silk,

cotton

and 'pétas'

The first hangings that were embroidered from the inside were in linen. Silk and Cotton were later used as supports for 'boutis' embroidery. The presence of hemp on the underside of some pieces deserves to be noted. If it is surprising to see it on the correct side on the other hand, then it confers to the rustic 'boutis' a whole dimension of unrecognised labour and an ancient quality that merits interest.

Silk

Asiatic origins

Behind the closed shutters, filtering the hot sun, in the shade of the thick walls of the 'bastide' and the 'mas', at the time of the siesta, in the coolness and in the shadowy light, the silk 'courtepointes' are sparkling and brilliant on the beds, setting fire to the divans and the layers of the occitan houses like fireworks. The bursting colours, taken up by our flags and banners, reds, blues and golds, proudly adorn the hallways of important people and the modest living places. The silk 'vanes' finely stitched, or embroidered in 'boutis', real treasures of patience buzz under the light caresses of delicate hands, as silk is precious.

Its history starts thousands of years ago, in the court of the Chinese Emperors. Light as thread it is a legend that no doubt came to us via the long caravans crossing Asia. The silk route and that of the spices ploughed their way through, making a passage to the shores of the Mediterranean. The secret of silk[1] was guarded within the high imperial palace walls for a long time. Emperor Fou-Hi would have tightened the silken threads on a celestial lyre himself, whilst his intelligent wife seized the opportunity for development as the breeding of the silkworm was born and developed in China. Reserved for the high dignitaries of the court, woven silk fabrics were to reach in stages only the Orient, and then the Occident. It is a Chinese princess who is supposed to be at the origin of the leak. Obliged to leave her country to marry a foreign king, she had the idea of taking a few mulberry seeds and a few silkworm cocoons with her hiding them carefully in her beautiful jet-black hair. Other stories tell of monks, around 500AD, having brought back the precious seeds in their bamboo canes… and so silk reached us.

In the Midi

The introduction of the silkworm in the Mediterranean countries was possible thanks to the culture of the black mulberry, which until then was growing wild. The abundant leaves on this Persian tree enabled the silkworm to eat. The installation of the Popes in Avignon encouraged the development of mulberry plantations in order to open up the possibilities of a textile activity of a new order. From the Renaissance onwards, this industry became one of the linchpins of the economy. All available money was put to work to improve production and create a qualified work force. Via the port at Marseilles, the raw materials were conveyed to the places of production or transformation. Marseilles had the right of taxing all merchandise which came through the port, causing the rise or fall of local industries. It was the richer classes who were persuaded by the kings to invest in these new industries. Work was no longer degrading for the nobles. Inventions and the organisation for the planting of mulberry trees and the plants for dying the fabrics were to improve the quality of the weaving, enabling new products to be created. At the same time, in every house, carding, threading and weaving took place either for personal use or for that of the merchants. The surplus was sold at the market.

As the silk worm heads towards adulthood, it spins a cocoon around itself. (Photographed at the Musée des Vallées Cevenoles at Saint Jean du Gard).

Following page
A bewitching, shimmering silk 'courtepointe'.

Fairs

Commercial exchanges took place at fairs and markets. The biggest specialised fairs, 'foires aux laines' (wool markets), animal markets and seasonal fairs drained off important crowds of merchants of all kinds, who came to buy and sell. Matters were negotiated once a year. The weekly or monthly markets which were held in the market or small towns attracted mainly farmers, who profited from the occasion by selling their farm products and in making a few clothing purchases. The wife would accompany her husband and purchase fabric sold by the 'canne', her provision of lace thread or handkerchiefs. The notoriety of the Beaucaire fair[2] is related in several stories by Frédéric Mistral, as well as in the archives relating to trading, which cannot be contested. Already, under Louis XI, its existence is mentioned, and it tells of its excellent situation. The privileges from which it benefits could not fail to attract the presence of several merchants. It is from the Renaissance onwards, from the 16th century, that the fair was to take on an international expansion. It was fundamental to business. Every year, during the third week of July, northern and southern Europe would meet there. For a few days, the cosmopolitan populations would mix, exchanging techniques and ideas. Between Provence and the Languedoc, Marseilles and Avignon, Beaucaire occupied a choice place. The swarming crowd of buyers would hurry onto the field where the fair was held along the banks of the Rhone. The entire Mediterranean assembled in this place where boats would discharge their spiced products from the Orient. Bundles of precious textiles and exotic perfumes were unloaded, causing huge confusion, an intense brouhaha.

Transformed into a real hive of activity, the streets of the town specialized in certain products: linen was sold in rue de Voiron, embroidery pieces and ribbons in rue des Quatre-Rois. In this third week of July, all the people living in the surrounding area came to live it up, the 'mas' became empty, as everyone was filled with wonder, concluding their business in the stands installed on the meadow.

The presence of several different textiles is brought back to the surface by studying the inventories. In the castles, precious fabrics were next to more ordinary fabrics. The noble lords appreciated cotton; beautiful stitched 'vanes' adorned the bedrooms of the castles.

Extracts from the inventory of François de Calvière, Lord of Boissières
(Gard, 1654 – Arch. Dép. 1082)

– 1 stitched quilted 'vanne', from Cadiz
– 4 Flanders tablecloths
– Set of bed linen of yellow burasse
– Set of Damascus linen – cover fringe in gold and silver
– Set of linen in yellow taffeta reinforced by 3 fingers + silk fringes
– Tapestries to decorate the bedrooms of Monsieur or Madame
– English silk stockings
– Stockings from Cadix
– 'Bazin' bonnets
– 12 tablecloths in 'cordat'
– Furniture coverings
– 'Couverture' in black bourazin

Extracts from the inventory of Rochemaure d'Aigremont

– A silk handkerchief
– 20 pairs of 'filoselle' stockings
– 8 pairs of white silk stockings
– 2 pairs of silk over stockings
– 1 pair of black silk stockings
– 2 silk 'couvertures'
– 5 stitched 'couvertures'
– 4 white stitched 'couvre-pieds'
– 3 'couvertures' of 'bazin'

Extracts from the inventory – Lord of Nogaret – February 1700.

– 121 sheets of different quality, fine or not
– 19 tablecloths
– 9 lots of a dozen fine serviettes
– 38 fine serviettes
– 45 thick serviettes
– 43 fine and new serviettes
– 15 shirts of 'limaçon', made in May, 1698
– 15 nuns' shirts
– Pewter service, marked with the name.

The service is marked with a name; on the other hand, the contents of the trousseau shows that thicker fabrics have appeared. The nuns' shirts are probably long nightshirts. The 'limaçon' fabric is doubly intriguing as firstly we know no meaning for the word, and secondly, why the particular care in specifying the date of the shirts' fabrication?

Preceding page: The fair at Beaucaire, famous throughout Europe, was the meeting place for the merchants and onlookers who came to 'live it up'. Musée Arlaten, Arles. Plate – J.L. Mabit, B. Delgado.

The silk fabrics of all colours used for 'couvertures', stockings and handkerchiefs are very rare, and rightfully appear in the wardrobes of both the well-to-do classes and the rich merchants.

Glory and commerce

Important centres were to develop the production of silk fabrics other than the hosiery business. In the south, Marseilles and Nîmes succeeded in creating beautiful fabrics in order to satisfy the demands of fashion and to respond to the luxury tastes of those who moved around more and more.

The woollen industry was on the decline. From 1560, this industry moved to the countryside, leaving the field wide open to the silk fabrics which established themselves in the cities. Nîmes and Marseilles argued over the market and claimed first place. In mixing the silk with the other raw materials of wool and cotton, Nîmes innovated and changed the quality, introducing 'little fabrics'[3] to the market of good value, the success of which helped to revive the regional economy. From 1726, the town specialised in the production of 'bourre de soie'. Thanks to its textile activities, at the end of the 18th century, Nîmes was assured the rank of 1st town of the Languedoc. Marseilles specialised in silk 'bourres' and 'bourrettes' from the grosgrain. Thanks to the spinning of the cocoons, 'filoseille' or 'bourrettes' were obtained. The fabrics, made from the grosgrain and then dyed, were used in the making of stitched silk 'courtepointes'. These ceremonial 'vanes' were made of silk fabrics on the top, and silk 'bourres' or linen on the underside. From 1685[4], 'courtepointes' were made of silk taffeta, an interior layer of silk wadding and a lining of taffeta. Their incredibly light quality (they weighed around 500g), and the quality of their stitching, were the factors that made them a success. The silk stuffing was of an incomparable softness, and was full-bodied; the extremely elaborate stitching, composed with brilliance and panache, was a mosaic of flowers. The whole piece had such a refined elegance that it could not but provoke an admiration that would never be denied.

Following page: marriage 'courtepointes' with identical motifs.

Forgotten jobs

Nîmes and Marseilles are two poles in the south, producing the same fabrics and garnishing the stitched 'courtepointes' stuffed with silk wadding. Languedoc and Provence perfected identical textiles and practised similar stitching techniques.

From the beginning, professions within the textile industry have mixed well with rural life. With insufficient revenues from agriculture, the profit made from working with silk made up the shortfall. In the family workshops[5] all sorts of silk fabrics were spun: stockings were made, as was 'cadis' in the past. These activities favoured the winter months. The names of the different jobs have almost disappeared, but out of the dust come documents and names, active in the past with their unknown tools, in front of strange jobs:

– Stocking makers[6] (or 'débassaïres)

– Makers of 'bourrette'[7]

– Silk 'chevilleurs': person who twinned two threads into one.

– Carders of 'filozelle

– Silk 'mouliniers': as 'chevilleurs', only of a higher grade, working in a mill.

– The makers of taffeta[8]

– The 'burataires' ('tisserand' – worker who makes thick fabrics in wool or in unspun silk.

A whole population comes out of the shadows to get to work on activities which seem foreign today. From the 'tisserand' to the embroiderer, the number of jobs that are connected to the textile industry is considerable.

Definition of the word 'bourre', taken from *Le Petit Robert*, and then translated:

– Bourre: coarse wool

– Bourre de soie: wastage after unwinding the raw silk bobbins.

– Bourre de laine: wastage from stitching the wool

– Bourre in the 18th century: coarse wool

– Bourre de coton: wadding

– La bourrette: coarse silk surrounding the cocoon

– Borretta: wastage of coarse silk (Occitan Dictionary)

Stuffed 'jupon' from Vaunage. This silk 'cotillon' was worn underneath the dress.

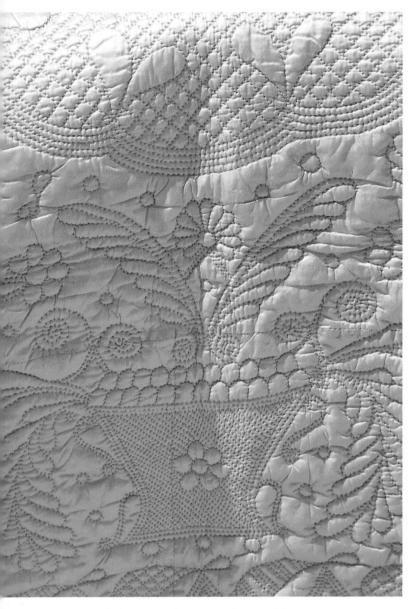

Straw baskets are overflowing with flowers and fruits, the symbols of prosperity.

Cape lined with silk.
The 'piqué' of the neck and hood gives elegance to the cape.
(Photographed at the Musée des Vallées Cévenoles at Saint-Jean-du-Gard).

Following page: Silk dress and stitched printed calico 'jupon'.
(Photographed at the Musée des Vallées Cévenoles at Saint-Jean-du-Gard).

On the ground, the organisation that was put in place so that profit could reach its maximum was remarkable. It was in several areas: the mulberry plantations[9] and their quality so that the greatest number of cocoons could be produced, the selection of silk worms so that the silk would be the most beautiful and the whitest, and a better qualification for the work force who, by training, would improve the technique and the supply of new tools. Conquering the marketplace was in the hands of the merchants, whose competence and daring opened up trade in Europe and the Americas.

All difficulties were overcome in spite of terrible outbreaks of plague in 1629, 1630 and 1720.

Subsidies were granted to motivate the farmers into planting different types of mulberries. Bonuses of 25 pounds per 100 feet have been quoted.

Marriage 'vane' of a traditional size, (1.5 m x 1.5 m). The central motif is from a sunflower. A crown of "boteh" (motif on Cashmere shawls) upsetting the balance of the minute square pattern.

The brotherhoods, corporations and those in charge of the law (jurande) controlled the jobs. Strict rules governed the organisation of work. The masters deepened their knowledge and passed it on to their colleagues and apprentices. The guild was an institution. It was very active from the 16th century and then again in the 18th. Teams were present in all areas of work. The emphasis was placed on values to be respected, such as work, education, art or wisdom. The young workers had to perform their tour of France[10], learning their trade from several masters around the country, staying a few months at a time. The guild proposed and led a serious apprenticeship with an objective of learning a high moral value. Art lessons, specific to each corporation, were organised so that each individual could complete a precise and carefully worked piece, as the jobs within the silk industry demanded a qualified work force.

Men possessing a certain education distinguished themselves in the silk industry. By their ingenuity and their knowledge, they found themselves project managers; their talents gave vigour to the industry. M. Paulet – designer and maker of silk fabrics – wrote and published in 1776[11] *L'art du fabricant d'étoffes de soie,* revealing his science. The work speaks highly of Claude Eymer[12], former merchant, who, due to his analytical and methodical mind was the head of a royal factory. François Traucaut[13], gardener at Nîmes, was at the origin of the first of the mulberry tree plantations. The particularly ingenious merchant-makers were to bring the products into focus, guarantee their entire fabrication and export them. It was they who orchestrated the whole regional economy. The fair at Beaucaire was the most important place for deals and business affairs and acted as a barometer for the economy. In order to gain from international trade, commercial dealings took place at Gênes and at Cadiz, thanks to the opening of family trading posts. Following the Revocation of the Edict of Nantes in 1685, the presence of exiled Protestants furthered exportation and the movement of new techniques. They helped to put an international business network in place.

In the diary of Abbot B-L Soumille[14] from Villeneuve-les-Avignon, there is a note in his handwriting that helps us appreciate the importance of silk at that time, and how a reputedly luxurious product could be introduced to the majority of houses:

"Scolastique and Thérèse have worn two town satin dresses, so goodbye to all dresses that are not silk, for as to our finery, we will not turn back." (Following mass given at the church at Domazan, 10th April 1746. Easter Day.)

Cotton

Not all the 'vanes' were made of printed calico, but almost all of them were stitched. Lawyers' deeds have given us a mass of information on textiles that were in the wardrobes of the 17th and 18th centuries. Three different periods followed one another – linen and wool, silk, cotton – with a transition period that was longer or shorter each time, marking the decline of the previous one, but never the complete disappearance.

Extracts from inventories

** De M. de Rochemore – Chateau de Monvert

– 8 cotton bonnets

– A suit of pink cotton velvet

– 3 'couvertures' of stitched 'bazin'

** De feu Antoine Dumas, the profit from his widow, Marie Foulc (1820)

– 1 cotton bed curtain in white squares

– 1 blue printed calico 'couverture'

– 2 pairs of cotton stockings

** De Marie Dumas, widow of François Fournier - Saint Côsme (1813)

– Set of bed linen in floral cotton fabric

– Bed curtain of printed calico

– Bed curtain of squared cotton fabric

** De … Sommières (1813)

– 1 printed calico 'courtepointe' with a leafy pattern

– 1 'courtepointe' of yellow cotton

– 1 'couvre pate' of printed calico

– 1 quilt (couvre pieds) of stitched 'bazin', sprinkled with flowers

From studying inventories 1, 2 and 3, it appears that cotton is present at all levels of society, in both clothes and household linens.

Silk, cotton and printed calicos were almost always stitched.

** De … Sommières (1813)

– 9 shirts of cotton percale chiffon

– 3 shirts of a white fabric

– 1 stitched quilt (couvre pieds) of cotton chiffon

Notice how the cotton is being reduced in colours and is in squares! As for the shirts, it was the cotton chiffons and the percales that were searched for.

From these different raw materials, it is clear that the workforce had to specialise and adapt to the new productions each time. Each new product modified in its own way the rules of trade that emanated from it and required improvements so that the economy would function at its best.

Cotton had been present in the kingdom since the Middle Ages. It was found mixed with other fibres, making 'basins', 'futaines' and 'cotonines'; in the trousseau, household fabrics and 'rouenneries' or 'rouan', were close to woollen fabrics, sheets and 'cadis'.

So for a few thousand years cotton has existed on several continents. Archaeological digs, remains and stories exist about this magic plant[15] which grows just as well in the valley of the Nile as it does elsewhere, in Africa, India, in the countries of the Orient and in the Americas; everywhere where the climate is favourable to its growth.

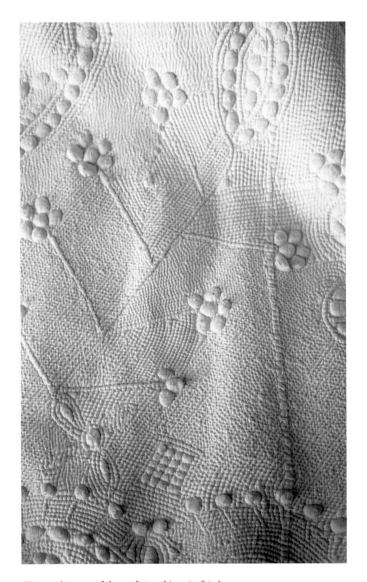

'Piquage' is part of the traditional 'savoir-faire'.

Triumph of cotton fabric

In the 17th century, cotton made a triumphal entry into the port of Marseilles in the form of printed calico - printed or painted fabrics coming from India. From that moment on a real revolution took place in the area with silk and wool relegated to second place. The preference for plant fibres was to be flaunted. The printing of bright colours, a price that everyone could afford and the easy upkeep of cotton were sufficient reasons to explain the public's infatuation with this new textile.

At the beginning, block printing was used on the fabric – fruitwood with the motif engraved on it. The choice of cotton to be used as the base support depended on which was the most suitable for this type of procedure, and moreover, which one responded best to the acids that fixed the colours. On the other hand, bleaching the fabrics meant that the quality of the results obtained were excellent. Year after year the use of cotton became more widespread. The town of Marseilles became a real little warehouse, as the raw material arrived there from India and the East, in "wool", that is to say in its untreated state, or woven. The woven fabrics were not only used in the making of printed calico, but also in the making of 'courtepointes', 'jupons', under-garments and household linen. The untreated cotton was spun and weaved in the area. Certain towns became important cotton centres, redistributing the work throughout the region: Montpellier, Marseilles, Nîmes, Avignon, Orange and Arles.

The "marchandise blanche"[16] – it is in this way that we label all white fabrics that are of a cotton or linen base – these finely woven fabrics are more refined, and because of this are more rare than ordinary cotton fabrics. In general, white is reserved for linens in contact with the skin: underwear, household linen and that of the trousseau. The colour of white hides a woman's modesty and is present in religious ceremonies.

Cotton became essential, and made all the structures that had been put in place for the silk industry tremble. Textile printing, copying that from India, was to take root in Marseilles and then be practised in the Midi area of France. The world, filled with wonder, discovered painted fabrics and its success was immediate. This new market was to pose a serious threat to the wool and silk markets. The all-powerful drapers and merchant-makers of silk put pressure on King Louis XIV to prohibit this market that was overshadowing theirs.

The first arrest was made in 1686. It was a period of prohibition. The wearing of printed calicos, of making printed calicos or of selling printed calicos was forbidden. From then on, the question should be asked, why create the 'Compagnie des Indes' in France, and prevent the sale of printed calicos, when England and Holland had their own companies, posing a serious threat to the French market? It is nonsensical to develop an industry to only then bind it hand and foot! Certain people saw within the ban a willingness to decapitate the Huguenot Diaspora, which, after the Revocation of the Edict of Nantes in 1685, threw itself into the making and selling of printed calicos[17]. Their emigration and their installation in Switzerland did not sway the king. Did these prohibitions hide a determination to ruin the economy of the Languedoc, the Mecca of the protestant religion?

Whatever the reason was, the quantity of cotton stored in the warehouses, the unemployment triggered by the slump of printed calicos from Marseilles, and the determination to give preference to cotton were reasons for the intensification of stitching techniques moving them towards what would become a decorative art all on its own: the 'boutis'. In 1743, an Armenian suggested installing cotton plantations[18] at Montpellier; others attempts were made in the Var, but the results were judged to be insufficient, so it was abandoned.

During this difficult period, contraband printed calicos were in circulation in the area. Aix was the linchpin. The ports of Rouen and Bordeaux, large importers of cotton, distributed the raw materials throughout France. The merchants of Marseilles were authorised to dispose of their stocks at the Beaucaire fair. The Midi region of France had sufficient white cotton fabrics to satisfy the making of traditional 'piqués' and the 'boutis' in particular. During this time, the printing of calico took place throughout Europe.

The cotton market was 'released' in 1759 with the raising of the ban. The manufacture of cotton fabrics underwent an important development. Thanks to the work-force, untreated cotton by the pound saw its value increase tenfold, as was the case for the cotton chiffons from Montpellier. From the moment the ban was raised the people of Nîmes sent a report to the general regulator, obtaining the freedom to paint and print on all sorts of fabrics as well as permission to import fabrics from India. The right to weave cotton was finally granted to the area in 1765, and the suppression of duties paid on cotton fabrics permitted the promotion of new factories. After 1780, spinning machines[19] were installed. Many manufacturers abandoned silk for the profit from cotton that was spun in the Cevennes, in the countryside, as long as they were weaving in the towns. It was still the agricultural population who made up the work-force.

Previous page: stitched printed calico 'cotillons' were the preference for a long time.

*The cotton has acquired
its nobility.*

Map showing the movement of cotton calico

**The route
of cotton calicos
from the 16th to
17th centuries**

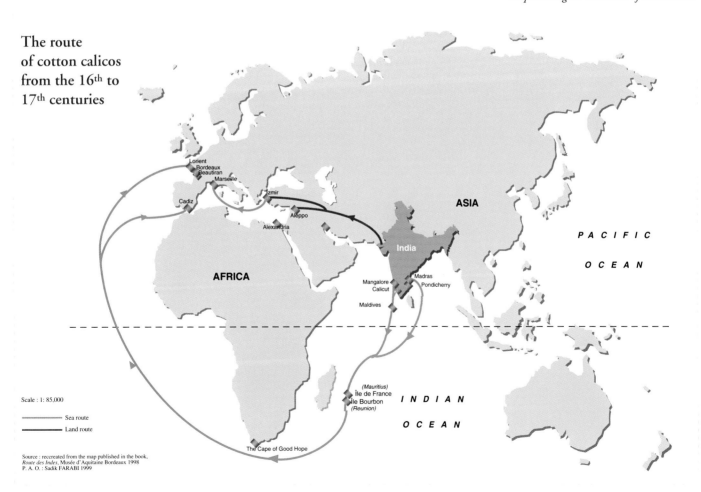

Lorient
Bordeaux
Beautiran
Marseille
Cadiz
Izmir
Aleppo
Alexandria

ASIA

India

PACIFIC

OCEAN

AFRICA

Mangalore
Madras
Calicut
Pondicherry

Maldives

(Mauritius)
Île de France
Île Bourbon
(Reunion)

INDIAN

OCEAN

The Cape of Good Hope

Scale : 1: 85,000

——— Sea route
——— Land route

Source : reccreated from the map published in the book,
Route des Indes, Musée d' Aquitaine Bordeaux 1998
P. A. O. : Sadik FARABI 1999

The royal manufacturers

When a factory aroused the attention of the king thanks to the excellence and originality of its products, it could hope to have the title of Royal Factory bestowed upon it. Having undergone a good many inspections and convinced the jurors of success and the profit that they could take from it, the factory would receive the title. To achieve this, it was necessary to react to high criteria, produce the most beautiful silks, the most beautiful cottons and the most beautiful dyes in order to attach this rare and enviable title to their factory.

In the 18th century, the Languedoc[20] possessed:
– 12 royal drapery factories
– 3 royal silk factories
– 2 royal cotton factories

Numbering only <u>two</u> royal cotton factories does not reflect the intense activity around this new industry, as it was given at the point when this blossoming trade was setting up, possibly before the lifting of the cotton tax which was later to open up the market. Other factories, however, which were not royal, enjoyed an excellent reputation and produced plain or printed cotton fabrics that were highly valued.

For example, at Nîmes, M. Eymar created a dyeing factory. Attaching a factory that made cotton fabrics to it, his establishment gained the title of 'Royal factory of dyeing, and of cotton fabrics'.

Recognisable by the sign of the royal arms and by the porter dressed in royal livery, these factories were granted special privileges. Jurors did not subject them to inspections. Within a predetermined radius around the factory, the workers could not work for anyone else, and they worked at a fixed salary … that is to say often a lower wage. On the other hand, they were forbidden from taking their knowledge and their work abroad.

The textile lords were all powerful. The regional economy depended on their savoir-faire and a qualified workforce at their disposal. Women and children participated in this economic outburst. The large fair at Beaucaire remained the principal distribution point of raw materials, finished products and played the role of economic barometer for all these industries. Other fairs and other markets distributed the merchandise. The archives from 1788 show figures of 44 fairs and 26 markets in the lower Languedoc. Peddling permitted novelties to enter the central countryside, despite impractical roads and paths.

'Courtepointe' of stitched cotton of "good colour" with the manufacturers label – Oberkampf. 1750 or 1758.

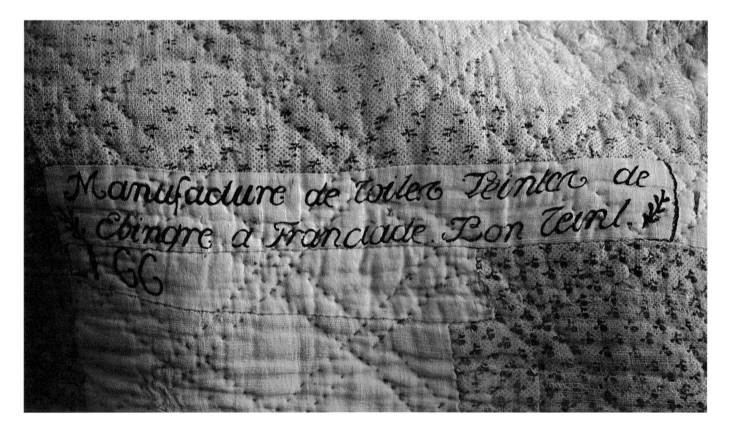

Stitched 'cotillons' of printed calico.

'Pétas'

The new and the old

If wool could not be used with the stitching techniques, then the opposite can be said of hemp fabrics, called household linens. They were used for table linen or the linen in the trousseau.

At the entrance to each village, the hemp field, cultivated by everyone, permitted the humblest of villagers to use the plants for their own linen. In the village, each peasant possessed a little plot destined for their personal use. The hemp and linen plantations permitted the production of fabrics that had plants at their origin, accompanying those made from wool. For a long time, this industry remained domestic. The country women combed the hemp and spun it with a distaff. The weavers made the fabric to order, when asked, to the requested width, often of four 'pans'. A 'pan' measured

approximately 25 centimetres, the distance between the thumb and the middle finger when stretched. The 'canne'[21] was another measure that was used and corresponds to 8 'pans' or 12 thumbs, which is about 2 metres.

The fineness of the fabrics, the grain being more or less coarse, depended on the spinner. The inventories showing the dowries of the girls who were to marry specify the quality and the colour of the fabric: in fact, white was rare and raised the value of the fabric. Years of washing were needed before a suitable white was achieved. Tablecloths and napkins of a grey fabric, mens' shirts whitened, bed furnishings in household linen, unbleached fabric to make sheets and 'cannes' upon 'cannes' of fabric as wedding presents: here is a precise language which paints a picture of the house by letting us see the intimate garments of the trousseaux of the time. The stories also underline the state of the linen: on the side of the new linens, there is always a whole range of words underlining the wear and tear. The old tablecloths, the inferior shirts, the patched stockings, the sheets from the old bed and the half

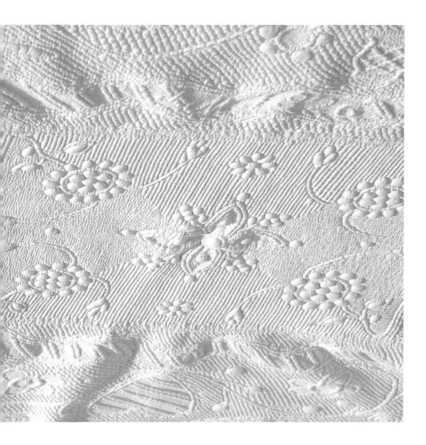

used mattresses were preciously kept and passed on in that state to the inheritor. Each inventory possesses its share of old rags or second-hand clothes.

An inventory from 1813 indicates a value on a batch of rags at 3 francs; in comparison, the price of a 'courtepointe' with a red leafy pattern was 6 francs. Therefore, a bunch of rags possesses a real value! The make-up of the trousseau reveals an importance that the girls, by the measure of their economies, did not hesitate to save for long in advance. Suzanne Peyre, in 1762, made up her dowry 'thanks to the savings that she made, working in dress-making since the death of her father', whereas Gabrielle Despuech, in 1778, acquired £90 of jewellery 'thanks to her savings and honest profits'. At the end of the 18th century, jobs that had until then been reserved for men were offered in the inheritance, permitting in this way an improvement to the standard of living, or to practise a profession: for example, a stage of spinning[22] in 1618, a job as a 'cadissier'[23] in 1766, a job as a 'molleton[24] in 1813, a job in 'bas'[25] in 1835.

Little 'vanon' made with different pieces of 'boutis' tastefully sewn together. (1826)

A 'vane' embroidered in 'boutis' made up of cotton 'lés' of different qualities.

Economising is a virtue

The use of patches then rags is almost banal but economising is the first virtue of housekeeping[26] as nothing should be thrown out. Scraps of fabric hide holes, or make up new cloth, from 'rags'. Women would patch, re-patch, alter, and 'hanter'[27] used sheets, re-knit the soles of stockings[28], alter clothes so that they were in fashion or to renovate a child's wardrobe. Patched materials were often used as linings for the wrong side of 'cotillons' and stitched 'couvertures'. The patch has a life of its own in which it either harmonises and melts into the other dyes or it stands out sharply in the most desperate of cases against the original colour as if to claim its right to exist. After 1789, many stitched 'cotillons' were often cut in two from the top, then put together to reconstruct new padded 'couvertures', in order to replace those requisitioned by the revolutionary armies. Everything that was padded was used, 'espeillé'[29], down to the marrow, the decorative function giving way to utility.

The 'piqués' were to finish their days in children's pushchairs in the guise of a mattress, on ironing boards to line the surface or as carpets for children, then when even more deteriorated, but still useful, in kennels or in agricultural sheds. An example of a 'couverture' patched, and re-patched, more and more worn, illustrates the obsessions and the practices of a period where economising dictated daily actions. The domestic preoccupations of society are perfectly illustrated by this re-use.

Certain 'boutis' have been kept intact, in their state, rigid in their beauty, sheltered from time, light and use, carefully folded inside household linens. Other families preferred to live with their 'boutis', placed here and there in their bedrooms, on furniture accompanied by misty eyed looks from their owners, caressed by knowing, caring hands. The bridal 'jupon', both padded and sewn in 'boutis', has also been made into little 'vanes'. Bits of 'boutis' fabric reconstruct the 'vanons' that decorate children's beds. The joining stitches are perfectly executed, more often than not, invisible, sometimes stuffed with tufts of cotton so that they melt into the background of the whole piece. When the motifs are joined up with happiness, the join does not appear.

Provencal Proverb

Dins li peio	*E dins li peioun*
In rags	*And in little rags*
Se nourrisson li belli filho	Li beu garçoun.
Pretty girls feed	*Handsome boys.*

Trésor du Felibrige. F. Mistral

Rags of kings

The nobles and the rich bourgeoisie also have their patches.

In Montvert castle, the armoires of the Baron d'Aigremont[30] contain, next to the luxurious fabrics, "old napkins and inferior sheets"; those of the Marquis d'Aubais[31] equally hold "old torn curtains, old tapestries worn through, cotton fabrics with holes and stitched 'courtepointes' made up of several pieces of fabric". His wife, Diane de Rozel, preciously preserved "a little bit of 'piqûre de Marseille'". The nobles really knew how to distinguish between the rich man's sheets, which were in linen, and those of the domestics, which were in unbleached fabric; they wore rich man's shirts of a fine bleached fabric, removed of their duvet[32]. The children from wealthier backgrounds wore 'brassières', corsets that were delicately worked in 'boutis', which were for the most part re-sized and reconstructed from the worn bodices or from 'chauffoirs' in 'piqûres de Marseille' or in 'broderie emboutie'. Recuperating beauty was the priority in these cases. The embroidery motifs in 'boutis' that have been saved were particularly well placed within clothing. The joins were invisible and melted into a decoration recomposed with taste and skill.

In wealthy families, it was frequent to reconstruct the childrens' undershirts from vermicelli 'boutis'.
Museon Arlaten, Arles. Plate J. L. Mabit, B. Delgado.

79

The white and the clean (la "bugade")

Such need and such love of linen could only be accompanied by proper, precise and effective actions, in order to look after and keep up this tradition that was attained at the cost of great effort.

Having been subjected to a soaking in bran water and several caustic washes, the fabrics were spread out in the meadow for several days. This bleaching process was followed by special washes called 'bugades'.

The 'bugade' consisted of washing the linen: that was the first part. The families in the 'mas', who did not have a washhouse, had large quantities of linen - from large trousseaux – as they only did their washing twice a year. It was rinsed in the river, often several kilometres away, with transport provided by their husband.

In the village, in her 'oustaou'[33], Rachel does her 'bugade' every month, at the changing of the sheets. She takes a large oak or zinc vat to put her linen in. When the vat is 'déglasi'[34] and the 'duelles'[35] fall inside, she wets it well in order to 'embuguer'[36] it so that the wood swells during the night. She puts her vat onto a tripod near the chimney and dresses it with a large 'bourin'[37]. She puts the dirtiest linen at the bottom: sheets, shirts, napkins and towels; then she pulls the 'bourin' over, having already slipped in a bouquet of bay leaves or lavender. She throws ashes on top from her favourite fruitwood. She waters her washing with warm water, catching the dirty water underneath from a hole in the base of the vat, and for several hours repeats the process.

Song of the 'bugadières' (washerwoman)
Found – both words and music –
by Lucienne Ortiz from Calvisson, Gard.

> *"C'est le jour de la lessive*
> *Pour les filles du hameau*
> *Et toutes, d'une allure fière,*
> *Marchent vers le bord de l'eau*
> *La corbeille sur la tête.*
> *L'on s'approche et l'on s'arrête*
> *On se dit bonjour gaiement…*
> *Ce tiède matin n'est-il pas charmant?*
> *Notre linge séchera pendant*
> *Que sur l'herbe on se lestera*

> "It's the day of the washing
> For the girls of the hamlet
> And all cutting a fine figure
> Walk to the water's edge
> Basket on their head.
> Approaching and stopping
> Saying gaily hello…
> This warm morning, isn't it charming?
> Our linen will dry whilst
> We lie down on the grass."

The washhouse in spring and summer, when the linen was rid of its impurities from the Marseilles soap, and having been vigorously hit with the 'battoir', was a reward. Whilst the washing was drying under the hot Midi sun, the women chatted and rested next to the empty wheelbarrows, in the shade of the large 'amouriés'[38].

Who can find a capable wife?
Her worth is far beyond coral.
She rises while it is still night…
…has no fear for her household when it snows,
for they are wrapped in two cloaks.
Her husband is well known in the city gate when he takes his seat with the elders of the land.
Excerpts from Proverb 31[39] from the New English Bible.

Cotton, silk and 'pétas' for all

Particularly in cotton and hemp, but also in silk, the techniques of wadding and of 'boutis' have vanished. All productions that enriched these textiles by stitching have touched every level of society, whatever their rank. The rich and the not so rich had their 'piqués'. It is curious to see the silk 'courtepointes' adorning the beds of the bourgeois and the nobility, but also, that a large place is given to cotton fabrics: 'basin' and printed calicos. The novelty of cotton, the infatuation of painted fabrics determined the choices made by the avant-garde minds. It is amusing to state that the subjects of Louis XIV made fun of the decrees and the bans, and that far from Versailles, each person did as he pleased, and slept under his 'vane' of stitched printed calico. The lower classes showed the same interests, but the proportions are the opposite: it was the cotton 'courtepointes', painted or not, that were in the majority; on the other hand, the feel of silk was present to maintain an enrichment obtained through trade or as the fruit of certain work. Every level of society implemented activities relating to supply or the making of fabric. Everyone knew how to establish hierarchies handing down the savoir-faire of handmade items. Until the 20th century, women, without being appointed, were closely linked to this textile industry as their participation was considerable, and they continued to practise it inside their houses, for their domestic needs.

Cotton 'boutis' seduce all generations.

Silk 'vane' monogrammed V.I. – R.D., embroidered in 'boutis' with symbols of the sun, hearts and birds. 1.25m x 1.45m.

Previous page: To know how to look after linen, to make it last, all comes from the competence of women.

81

NOTES

1. See *Les chemins de la soie* – Espaces Écrits.

2. The Fair at Beaucaire – Arles exhibition catalogue, 1999.

3. See article by Martine Nougarède, curator of the 'musée du vieux Nîmes', catalogue for the Arles Exhibition, 1998.

4. Date mentioned by the Arch. dép. of Provence.

5. See article by Martine Nougarède, curator of the 'musée du vieux Nîmes', *Au fil de temps* (14.06 and 27.10.1991).

6. Faiseurs de bas, faiseurs de bourrette, taffetassiers: see *Trois siècles d'ascendance nîmoise* by J.Crye-Fenouillet. Ass. Artistique de la banque de France. Section on Genealogy.

7. Ibid.

8. Ibid.

9. *L'Industrie de la soie en Bas – Languedoc XVIIᵉ et XVIIIᵉ siècles*, Line Tesseyre – Salhman.

10. Arch. Dép. BR.1674 – PER. C. 31/1993. In the list of Corporations de Nîmes, made in 1767, the corporation of 'taffetiers' and makers of silk fabrics had 450 masters.

11. See catalogue of the exhibition, 1998, Arles, Martine Nougarède.

12. Highly praised by Monsieur Phélip (1822), former merchant, member of the 'Académie du Gard'.

13. François Traucaut: *Nos garrigues et les assemblées du desert* – Dr Albert Domergue – Presses du Languedoc – Max Chaleil, editor.

14. Diary of Abbot B-L de Soumille: Arch dép. du Gard – B.H. 1017.

15. As it was called in Syria. See (*Syrie, signes d'étoffe* – House of World Cultures – A.C.L. Éditions 1988, Société Crocus).

16. 'La marchandise claire' or 'la marchandise blanche' encompasses a whole range of fabrics which make you dream, for example, 'la mousseline claire, le lizat (lisat), le nansouque (nansouk), les batistes, les toiles fines de Rouen, des Indes, les percales de Pondichéry'. 'Lizat' is a fine white cotton fabric, from India, and was used in the fabrication of 'couvertures' stitched in Marseilles. (Katsumi Fukasawa, *Toiles et commerces du Levant, d'Alep à Marseille* – Paris 1987).

17. On the fabrication of printed calicos, see the catalogue of the Arles exhibition 1999.

18. Annie Roux, *Le textile en Provence* – Edisud.

19. On the spinning machines, see Arch. Dép du Gard – DUTIL M 7948.

20. Factories of the Languedoc, see Arch. Dép du Gard – DUTIL M 7948.

21. A 'canne' is a measure quoted by Annie Roux in, *Le textile en Provence* – Edisud.

22. A stage of spinning: wedding of Magdaleine Cardenousse – 13 Dec. 1618, Genealogy of Mme R. Verdier – Saint Cômes et Maruejols.

23. A job as a 'cadissier': inventory from the death of Ch. Arjalais – Genealogy of Mme R. Verdier – Saint Cômes et Maruejols.

24. A job as a 'molleton': wedding of Suzanne Tesse – Aujargues (the area around Sommièresis renowned for the making of flannelette).

25. A job in stockings: wedding of Boissonat Suzanne – Saint – Dionizy – Gard.

26. See *En jupon piqué et robe d'indienne* – M. Biehn – éd. J. Lafitte.

27. The central part of a worn sheet was removed and placed at the edge. In this way, the sheet would last longer.

28. See the article by the author in *Rosalie, Léa, Émilie, Éva et les autres*. Éd. Bouchardeau.

29. 'Espeillé' – transformed into rags, in bits.

30. The Baron d'Aigremont: inventory of Montvert Castle, 1785.

31. The Marquis d'Aubais: inventory of Charles de Baschi, 1777, by Mathias Baron-Martel. Arch. Dép du Gard – Municipal Archives, Aubais.

32. Cotton canvasses underwent, with the bleaching, cutting or burning of the downy vegetable hair. Annie Roux, *Le textile en Provence* – Edisud.

33. 'Oustaou': village house, tall and narrow, often two stories, with a shed/workshop on the ground floor.

34. When the vat is empty, the duelles (wooden sections of the barrel) would fall inside.

35. Parts of the wooden vat that were rounded.

36. Soaking the vat (if it is wooden) in water when dry, so that it would become watertight.

37. A sort of coarse sheet in 'toile de ménage' (cleaning cloth).

38. Mulberry trees, called the trees of love.

39. "The life of Rachel", by the author, *Rosalie, Léa, Émilie, Éva et les autres*. Éd. Bouchardeau. Biblical proverb quoted by Renée Verdier in *Femmes aux champs*.

Bibliographical references relating to the silk industry, taken from the Departments' Archives at Nîmes.

– Rendre au travail sa noblesse : Chambre des métiers - BR. 1168.

– Liste des corporations - 1767 - Gaston Mamejols - BH. 1033.

– La gomme :

Arts industriels proposé par M. Fauquier - Capitaine du génie.

Les foires - PER C. 14/1989.

1990.

– Beaucaire XVIIᵉ siècle : BH. 1113.

PER. C. - 64/1990.

PER. C. - 43/1976.

PER. C. -12/1989.

BR. 443.

– Beaucaire XVIIIᵉ siècle :

BH. 1193

PER. C. 89. 1993. Uzès.

Arts et métiers.

– Sommières :

PER. C. 77. 1995.

BR. 61.

BR. 348.

– Compagnons:

PER. C. 31/1993.

– Procédés de décruage de la soie:

PER. C. 1/1832.

– Les compagnons du tour de France du XVIIᵉ siècle à nos jours:

BR. 1674 - Paul Marcelin.

– DUTIL Léon :

C/3/21.

M/7948.

– Annales du Midi : PER. C. 3/1905.

– 35 J 21.

– 35 J 57.

– Industrie :

BR. 1861.

BR. 2074.

BR. 1954.

PER. C. 55/1985.

Distinctive workshops

Light and shadow in the Petite Camargue

At the entrance of the Petite Camargue, a few steps from the lagoons that border the Mediterranean Sea, where the cracked earth touches the water, where the vegetation diminishes, becoming the 'sansouîre', the 'boutis' was completed in a different way.

While the men occupied themselves with tending the animals – horses and bulls – in their herds or working on the vines, the women, such as Penelope, threw themselves during the evening hours into their time consuming, exquisitely fine needlework. They are so easily recognisable as all is light and transparent on these 'vanes'. The light and graceful shadows of the stitched bouquets outline in filigree the ethereal elements. These 'vanes' embroidered in the Marsillargues region (Hérault) have all the same characteristics. They are achieved from two well-established models, only two of which exist in a perimeter of a few kilometres, which leaves us to think that there must be a workshop in the village or its surroundings. Naturally, some questions come to mind: did the women have the right to create a new design? Were there any constraints, rules that had to be respected, as there were in the guilds? Were there laws that regulated production? Everything is left to contemplation, as these repetitions are not the fruit of chance. On the other hand, the quality of the stitching varies from one piece to the next, which confirms that there were several 'piqueuses' as opposed to one in charge of a repetitive work.

However, the development of the central medallion shows the personal creation where the young girl's initials were sometimes embroidered. A garland of packed leaves crisscrossed, undulating near the straight borders and the corners are perfectly identical, something that isn't always the case. There are other cases of pictures: the parity of the motifs two by two and conflicting following the diagonal, or even the four corners. Three 'palms' from the mimosa occupying the space, the beads representing the flowers scattered as in a game of skittles, whilst on the sides the slightly angular shanks, similar to the clusters of saladelles – a flower of the Camargue region - stretch out to infinity. In the other model, the branches stream forth from a little cauldron. We recognise, on the sides of the cauldron, the two handles by which it is to be held. Is it not the cauldron that is always hanging in the fireplace in the dairy? It is highly possible, as it was the practice in the Midi to dry the sacred plant of the herdsman in order to brighten up a chilly winter.

In these two cases, we find the same paving in the background, the same little drawings, but placed in different areas. The vermicelli are absent, but to keep the fabric taut, motifs are stitched though not stuffed. This method of fabrication appears in principle on certain pieces of 'boutis' embroidery on which the base was sprinkled with random stitches or French knots.

This workshop had a certain influence. The destruction of the archives in a fire makes research difficult, but surrounds the history in a mystery which suits the 'boutis'.

Marriage 'vane' (1.54 metres by 1.55 metres, initialled A.L. from Marsillargues. Adélaïde, Louche, born 18.10.1829 at Marsillargues. Composition and typical corner motifs; in this type of work, transparency was a privilege.

Marriage 'vane' initialled V.L., originally from Marsillargues. The centre is lightly wadded. The design is identical to one on another 'courtepointe'.

Corner of a traditional 'courtepointe' with a bouquet – supposedly – of a mimosa, (due to the bunches of flowers.)
On the exterior, the fine stems evoke the salicorne of the petit Camargue.

Sculptures in fabric from the land of the Marquis

A few kilometres from there, Vauvert stretches out into the vines like a large toad. We are in the country of the Marquis de Baroncelli, in the country of the 'biou' - nickname for the bulls - on the edge of the Petite Camargue. Within a few minutes the countryside changes, reeds and tamarisks share a land of meadows, lagoons and dry, arid earth. The sea covered this whole stretch four thousand years[1] ago. On pulling back, leaving this land saturated by salt, the sea favoured the salicornia shoots, filarial and 'restincle'[2] bushes. The Phoenician juniper, a magical tree of the Camargue, bears with great pride large red fruits here. In this countryside, the herdsman is king. One lives and breathes the 'bovine'. The Marquis, through the Nacioun Gardiano that he founded in 1904, strongly impregnating the life of the whole region, revived the traditions and the bull games. The creation in 1512 of the Old Brotherhood of Herdsmen in Arles bears witness to the antiquity and the importance of these traditions across the centuries.

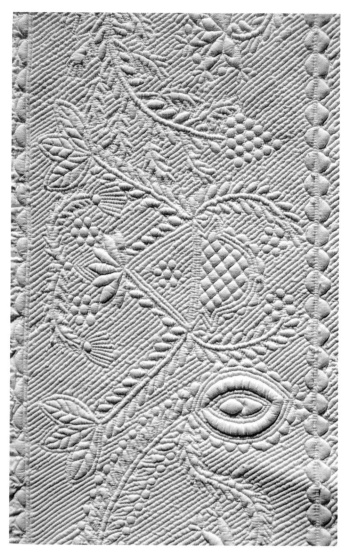

Detail on a bridal 'jupon' with a consistent relief. The cauldron is bordered by leaves between a bunch of grapes and a fruit which could be garlic.

The embroidery gives lightness to a 'boutis' of which the relief was one of the particularities of the region.

From Vauvert to Nîmes, the boutis were fashioned with the same ardour. In the eyes of their fellow workers who worked on the 'bas-relief' – sculpted panels from the bible - and on the stone cathedral tracery, the women chiselled even the smallest piece of their 'boutis' to make genuine miniatures. Here with airy transparency it was the play of light on the work that altered the relief of the design every second. The back stitch, previously used by men of art[3], was conserved and used judiciously on certain surfaces, those which were to be highly valued. A particular form of packing accompanied this technique. The association of these two particularities, heightened by the sliver of an openwork embroidery stitch, was the sign of savoir-faire above the norm, the signature or paw print of a master. The whole piece shows the spirit of a certain guild.

The values of the whole region declined in this tradition; our boutis breathed of everything that we had in the past.

They are the witnesses of man's life, steeped with the scent of our houses from many generations. When necessary, we know to keep a few little secrets in order to preserve objects that show the individuality of each little area of the Occitan region. In the guild, it was the custom to progress or be promoted according to ability and merit. To climb to the highest level of knowledge, having proved oneself is a logical step, one which deserves to be respected, and brings us back to the present day.

The official documents of the town hall in Vauvert, as well as those in the county archives in Nîmes, do not contain information to help us pinpoint the precise location of the workshop. However, the presence of a certain Flandin, state taffeta merchant, whose signature appears at the bottom of every civil state document, as does that of Joseph Roux, merchant, tightens the thread around a textile industry existing within the village.

How is it that workshops so close to one another can have ways of doing things that are so different from one another, and yet it is still correct to find similarities in the way that the 'vane' is made, or in the end-product? It is clear that each workshop possessed its own designs – ordered possibly from the same artist – and that the choice and the quality of the design depended solely on the financial means. In the system of guilds and brotherhoods, the laws and rules that governed the organisation of the workshops did not permit the transmission of secrets regarding their own particular knowledge. Individual freedom was limited.

We have no choice but to question the originality of the designs when there is the repetition of the same motif in precisely the same location. We understand that in certain cases the designs could have circulated in an enlarged area, notably on the 'jupons' of the bride and the 'pétassons' lent from woman to woman; but the 'vanes' created in these workshops are important both in number and within the small area that they exist. Therefore the designs were not freely circulated. Until the 19th century, men monopolised all areas of work. They held the wheels of commerce and manufacture in their hands. The arrival of women in jobs associated with couture appeared officially in 1667 during the reign of Louis XIV.

Women were only underlings, who worked in the same manner as adolescents, and could do so only if they were widows.

Ceremonial 'pétasson'. The 'boutis' sculpts the fabric and is adorned with little jewels in embroidery which mark the identity of a specific area.

The mystery of the designers

It is always around the royal manufacturers that the best designers are found, and in the entourage of the king. In order to obtain the title of 'royal' the manufacturers associated themselves with designers, well-known artists. The best ones were to be found at the Gobelins, in Paris, and in the large towns where industry or the arts prospered: Lyon and Marseilles distinguished themselves because of their painting schools or academies. The models used for the manufacture of the boutis have not been found; the stencils and the perforated pieces of paper that exist could have been used for embroidery but not for the boutis. The lack of documentation is cruelly felt and touches all the arts; the difficulty in preserving the models through the centuries, their destruction through the emptying of attics leaves a hole difficult to fill. An engraving by Arthur Grenard[4] of the royal workshops depicts a painter in front of his easel sketching a panel of arabesques with the engravers surrounding him ready to leap in when the drawing is complete. Réveillon, a designer and creator of wallpaper, employed a number of designers for his creations; the list of personnel making the wallpaper numbers two, without giving names. Only the great masters, recognised the majority of the time by the royal authority, had the right to be named. In 1795, the workshop of Jacquemart and Benard employed two chief designers to annually update the papers and colours.

Whatever we think, textile designers are quite rare and look for their inspiration from the painters. At the same time, these painters were sought to become directly involved in decoration. In the 18th century, the success of Jean Rodolphe Wetter[5] and of Christophe Philippe Oberkampf in printing calico was built on the excellence of their designs.

Spirit of India on the base of a 'jupon', transformed into a 'couverton' inspired by motifs from cotton calico.

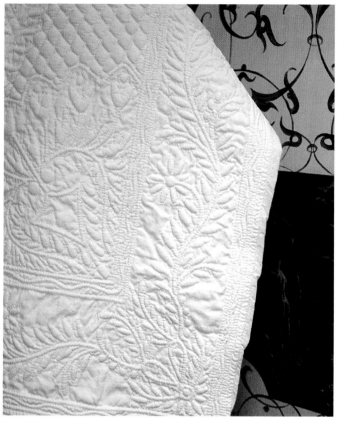

Curls and arabesques on a 'boutis' and painted furniture.

The composition, the designs, and the size of these silk 'vanes' are identical. Miniscule modifications on the level of the details show that care has been taken to not totally reproduce the same model.

Famous Collections

Still in the 18th century, Jean Pillement, the author of *Fleurs idéales,* illustrated and created in 1763 floral compositions with Chinese ornaments, in an Indian style. During the Century of Light the famous painters were talking about them: Joseph-Laurent Malaine, flower painter for the king and Berain, designer to Louis XIV. The presence of famous artists in the provinces, their style copied and adopted by their numerous students, can be seen on the fabrics but also on the wall hangings, the silver plates and the china. They

were ornaments capable of being adapted to demand. The princes and the nobles, imitating the King, threw themselves into constructing a mini Versailles, welcoming the plethora of artists who travelled from court to court, contributing to the renewal of the arts.

In textiles the clientele became hard to please, demanding that models be revamped. At least once a year, in order to satisfy the needs of fashion, the true professionals had, as their mission, to create new designs. They interfered in the production between the conception and the final product. The silk or painted calico worker became merely a means to an end. A control on the subject of designs for fabrics was put in place in 1787. In spite of this, the institution of registration was created on 19th July 1793. The need for designs was only growing in order to satisfy an increasingly demanding market. Correspondence between manufacturers and designers existed and shows the necessity of variety in design. In Nimes, Master Paulet, designer and maker of 'silk fabrics', was upset and would have liked his pupils to go to Lyon for their apprenticeship, as the town possessed the silk merchants, just as in Marseilles, he had his art school.

In the 16th century, the first books containing designs were created out of planks of engraved wood. With the invention of printing, the collections created by the Italian artists began to circulate in the royal courts and the renowned manufacturers. These collections were greatly appreciated.

L'Esempio di recammi de Giovanni Tagliente (Venice 1527) or *Le livre nouveau pour patrons de lingerie* published by Pierre de Sainte-Lucie in Lyon between 1530 and 1533 were distributed as many examples. When models were not being created, the artist was simply invited to stay at the chateau. When there, he created even more.

The motifs are traced directly onto the 'clean fabric'. Catherine de Medici had 321 squares of embroidery, 538 pieces of patterned fabric of all sizes, some long pieces of golden fabric with the embroidery already started, strips of gauze upon which the motif was already drawn in her coffers. In 1626, the painter Quentin Warin was very taken with this type of creation and contributed to it, to the supremacy of certain convents, notably to those of the Ursulines. The inventories of noble families underline, completely, the presence of pieces of embroidered tapestry. In the wardrobes at the chateau d'Aubais, in the trunk marked no.2, were 34 pieces of embroidered tapestry in silk and wool of which two were the

Marriage 'courtepointe' (1.22 metres by 1.50 metres.)
Originally from Milhaud. Remarkable because of its relief and composition.
Around a central medallion, bordered with acorns, the bouquets
in the corners flow out of Medici vases. The stems of the flowers mix
harmoniously with the wheat. Abundance, prosperity and
longevity can be extricated from the chosen, but sober ornamentation.

coat-of-arms for M. le Marquis and the other 32 were for beds, chairs and stools.

The procedure of noting down the designs required first of all the creation of a scaled model on a large piece of paper, in either lead or burnt reed. Thanks to a sheet of paper coated with soot slid underneath the motif, the design of the model was transferred to a plank of wood. The person responsible for the laying out of the wood intervened and with the help of a spike followed the contour of the motif, which then appeared on the wood. The engravers "en taille douce"[6] were then to scratch out the channels which would permit, with the help of swabs, the printing of the motifs. The difficulty was in resolving the matter of cutting out the motifs, as the planks were no more than 50 cm long, and in marrying the joins. The planks then made possible the reproduction, to the point of infinity, of the ready-to-use stencils. This procedure of 'taille douce' was to be used for a long time in all the arts: tailors, craftsmen in ironwork, cabinetmakers, calico printers and the makers of 'boutis'.

NOTES

1. Date mentioned by C. Martin in 'L'île de Camargue'.

2. Camargue vegetation.

3. Under Louis XIV, they were professional embroiderers.

4. Arthur Grenard Manufacturers: see 'Papiers peints en arabesques'.

5. Designers and 14 engravers.

6. See 'Les Arts Décoratifs en Provence', Edisud. At the end of the 17th century, in the printing of calico, a contract of association to print 'en taille douce' all sorts of images was concluded between Louis David, originally from Vincennes, and Antoine Coutelet from Avignon.

Workshop of the tailors.
Museon Arlaton, Arles, Plate J.L. Mabit, and B. Delgado.

Motifs
and symbols

Art in everything

The artistic movement, at the time of the Italian Renaissance, was to touch France and flourish under Louis XIV during the Century of Light. At this time the Academies of Art were blossoming in the large towns. In the schools, the celebrated artists – established to practise the major arts represented by painting, sculpture, and architecture – did not deign to use their talents to the service of the other more secondary arts. The mix within business meant that democracy came to the fore and beauty entered into the houses of the bourgeois, adorning the walls with hangings, sculpting the 'courtepointes' made in 'pîqures de Marseille'. Furniture was painted and the painted calicos from the textile industry were to undergo a dazzling development, due to new techniques.

The unchanging success of antique art and exotic perfume, brought in the sails of the large caravans from India and the East, were to contribute to the mix of styles. The artists possessed a great number of Greek/Roman motifs; they studied the loges of the Vatican, decorated by Raphaël; they knew the Lyon silk factories; they drew from the repertoire of printed calicos and from Persian fabrics[1] with inspiring arabesques woven on Oriental rugs. They possessed the facilities to gather all the styles and use them according to the taste of the period. Their files overflowed with sketches, outlines and works of art, their documentation covered a large range… Files of drawings could be bought.

Photograph, page 94: Wedding 'vane', (1.42 metres by 1.55 metres) in piqué de Marseilles. The ensemble is solemn thanks to an antique demonstration. The cornucopia symbolises prosperity, fertility and happiness. The temple, surrounded by people, is a reflection of the divine world.

The search for artistic emotion across a balanced harmony of shapes.

The similarity of certain designs would lead one to believe that there was a certain bond between manufacturers of different styles. The example quoted by M. Jacqué – curator of the wallpaper museum at Mulhouse – on the subject of common themes at Réveillon[2] and Oberkamp[3] confirms these hypotheses.

A corner of a 'courtepointe' where the harvests are present: wheat and flowers, artichoke or acanthus leaves, basket of melons. The base is a fundamental motif to the construction of the arabesque. It serves as a departure point for a motif that opens out, garnished with acanthus leaves. Composition with a harvest bouquet: wheat, daisies and leaves.

96

In the Century of Light

On the stamped embroideries, the flowers, beautiful as they are, were not thrown at random onto the fabric in improvised armfuls. Equipped with a keen sensitivity for the arrangement, the designers were capable of putting pleasantly together several motifs, even if they took no notice of the size of the ornaments, as, in the 17th century, it was the piece that dictated all.

The collection of plant designs for the embroidered 'boutis' pieces devoted a large section to Acanthus leaves and ornamental boughs coiled into branches, with motifs that were pleasant and agreeable to the eye. The arabesque theme[4] was to be used successfully again and again in all the decorative arts, until the 20th century. Entwined in this greenery, were birds, including parrots, eagles, peacocks and above all, a pair of pigeons, all in the taste of the period. Moreover, subjects in this repertoire are found across all the arts.

During the Century of Light, in the textile industry, floral art remained the preferred subject. Introduced by the Jesuit priests in the 16th century in the courts of the Mogul kings[5] in India, the printed calicos – painted fabrics – reproduced the flowers of the herbarium. Imagine how these French flowers, dried and flattened, with bits missing, must have seemed strange to the artists who were drawing them. These flowers, which were to serve as models in the same way as theirs, returned to France, painted on fabrics, printed by planks of wood. It was magical. Filled with wonder, France had discovered printed calico, and, after its huge success, Marseilles reproduced them from 1640[6], improving the techniques and colours. The European fashion had begun. When the ban was introduced in 1686, the factories conserved and intensified the 'pîqures de Marseille', embroidery and other stitched creations. White or single coloured cotton supported this, while the motifs for the printed calicos were used for other purposes rather than printing.

Progression of printed calico across Europe during the 17th and 18th centuries

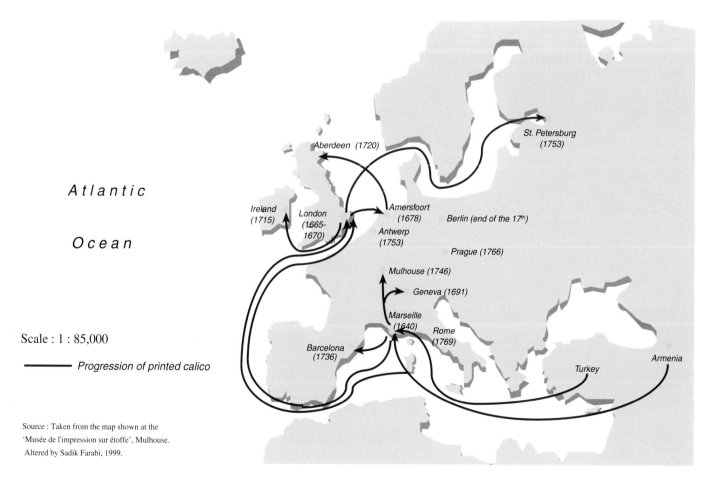

Atlantic

Ocean

Scale : 1 : 85,000

———— Progression of printed calico

Aberdeen (1720)

St. Petersburg (1753)

Ireland (1715)

London (1665-1670)

Amersfoort (1678)

Berlin (end of the 17th)

Antwerp (1753)

Prague (1766)

Mulhouse (1746)

Geneva (1691)

Marseille (1640)

Rome (1769)

Barcelona (1736)

Turkey

Armenia

Source : Taken from the map shown at the 'Musée de l'impression sur étoffe', Mulhouse. Altered by Sadik Farabi, 1999.

What became of these motifs over time, and what remains of them?

From the collections studied, the known motifs were catalogued enabling classifications to be established. Several years of contacts, meetings, studies and research have helped to establish this inventory. Without doubt, it will be necessary to follow up certain elements as the real 'boutis' are still consigned to the ranks of a secret heritage. Information is still sparse, and to this day does not permit a complete understanding of the collection of illustrations. Will it always be so? It is not always possible to put a name to a flower which has been embellished by its raised quality, but at the same time deformed.

And so it is on the ground of the lower Occitan region, in the towns, villages and countryside, in the chateaux and the farmhouses that the following motifs were itemised.

By way of explication, frequency and durability of the motif was taken into account in the making of these tables.

Harmony and grace burst forth from amphora vases and dance a choreography that celebrates power and glory.

98

A voyage through time

– 14th century

Pieces of 'piquées' are present in princely inventories where the technique is closest to that of the 'boutis'. They are in linen and stuffed with coloured wool.

The motifs belong to a picture book illustrating successive scenes in the form of a list, which tells the stories of Tristan and Isolde, Solomon or Alexander the Great.

– 16th century

A large green and natural coloured 'courtepointe' of silk and cotton has been found that was made in the Indies for an imperial family. It was an order placed either from Italy or from the House of Austria.

The right side of the piece is in ivory silk and the underside is of green cotton.

The piece in question portrays, in succession, a naval battle (4 caravels), a hunting scene in a forest (with both real and fantasy animals), and flowering archways brought to life with people.

– 17th century: The Century of Light: Louis XIV – Louis XV

On the studied pieces, lots of flowers from the Indies can be found, and the taste of the time was also for the exotic Iznik faiences. We can equally admire the luxuriant plant compositions, Medici vases, branches with or without leaves, pearls, palms and grapes.

– 26th October 1686

Printed calico was prohibited. Veto on the making, selling and wearing of them.

– 1755 –1759: The Directory

Placing of the baskets or the flower bowls in the centre of the 'vanes', with a more natural floral repertoire.

The initials of the maker are found in a medallion.

– 1759

Removal of the veto: the sale of printed calico is authorised.

– 1789: The French Revolution

Requisition of all 'couvertures piquées'

– 1804 – 1814: 1st Empire – Napoleon 1st

Particularly prized motifs: laurel wreath and garlands, olive garlands, bees, the use of vermicelli and, for the bottom, the floral composition.

– 1814 – 1848: Restoration – Louis XVIII

Vases, signs, urns, cornucopias, and flowering baskets were all to be found.

– 1852 – 1870: Second Empire

European and exotic fruits and flowers were the most popular subjects.

– Second half of the 19th century

The 'natural' collection grew bigger: fruits (melons, grapes), southern French flowers, wild flowers, vegetables, roosters, pairs of birds and hearts.

The last known 'boutis' dated 1869.

This chronology is relative as all the types, styles and fashions continued to be used long after they had made their first appearance.

A theme that was successful was never abandoned.

There are re-occurring themes – the vine, for example – which was used in every period.

To date a piece of 'boutis', several elements must be considered:
– The collection of illustrations,
– The composition,
– The border,
– The stitches used,
– Specific motifs.

Imperial eagles, (Napoleonic period.)

Medallion monogrammed P.R.

Collection of illustrations

(This is not an exhaustive list, as over several years, the author has added to it from her studies and research.)

Code used

P .... on the 'Pétasson'
V .... on the 'Vane'
J .... on the bridal 'Jupon'
C .... on the 'Coussinière'

Motifs used on printed calico

(For comparison with those used on the 'boutis')

Roses .... Tulips .... Primroses
Lilacs .... Lily of the Valley .... Hollyhocks
Cornflowers .... Ear of Corn .... Grasses
Bulrushes .... Fruits .... (peaches and pomegranates)
Peonies .... Poppies .... Irises
Madder Flowers .... Garlands of Flowers .... Hyacinths
Magnolia .... Chrysanthemums .... Orchids
Lotus Flowers .... Plumes .... Cherubs
Sweet Williams .... Palms

The wild flowers were inspired by the motifs from India
(Indiano Piso).
Garden flowers, seedlings from the wild flowers
and slightly darker fabrics.
The insects: butterflies, dragonflies, and flies.

*(This collection of illustrations comes from collections
of printed calicos and from the books in the bibliography.)*

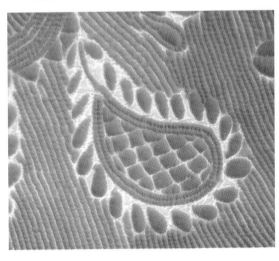

*The 'boteh' is an indo-Persian motif,
(small palm,) lightly curving in towards the top.*

*Tulip styles inspired the vermicelli 'boutis' of
the seventeenth century. Repertoire of oriental earthenware.*

Motifs carved on regional furniture

Breadbin – Salt box – Carpet beater

Roses . . . . Tulips
Baskets . . . . Olives
Wheat . . . . Fish
Harpoon . . . . Net
Sun symbols

Traditional 'Armoire' – Chest of drawers

Baskets . . . . Tureens
Pearl necklaces . . . . Initials
Reeds . . . . Artichokes
Acanthus leaves . . . . Ears of corn
Tulip . . . . Rose
Cornucopia . . . . Pairs of birds
Pearls . . . . Flaming torches
Quiver and arrows

On bulbous clocks
Thistles
Pairs of birds

Popular motif sculpted on furniture, showing the same inspiration as those done on the 'boutis'.

Motifs on the 'boutis'

Cultivated flower

Flowers from Indies and Turkey	V, J.
Tulips + leaves	V, J.
Roses + leaves	V, J.
Peonies + leaves	V, C.
Sunflowers	V.
Lilac	V, C.
Peonies	V.
Indeterminate flowers	on everything.
Lily	V.
Sweet Williams + leaves	V, J.
Rosebuds	V, J.
Rosettes	V, J.
Thistles + leaves	V.
Bell shaped flowers (acanthus?)	V.
Hydrangea + leaves	P.
Lupins	J.
Fritillary	J.
Dahlia	V.

Wild flowers

Corn Poppy	V, J.
Daisy	P, J, V.
Meadowsweet	J, P.
Violet	J.
Convolvulus	V.
Dandelion	V, J.
Wild Iris	C, V.
Horsetail	V.
Dog Rose	C.
Bluebells	V.
Cornflowers	C, V.
Rosemary	V.
Bramble flower	C.
Vine flower	V.
Madder flower	V.
Colocynth	V.
Mallow	V, J.
Marguerite (large Camomile)	V, J, P.
Buttercups	C, V.
Catchfly	V, J.
Periwinkle (mark of Solomon)	V, J.
Primrose or Cowslip	J.
Star Anise	V, J, C.
Pomegranate flower and bud	V.
Corn Campion	J, V.
Wild Azalea	J, V.
Wild Grasses	V.
Wild Garlic	V, J.
Flax	J, V.
Glasswort	V.
Turk's-cap Lily	V, J.

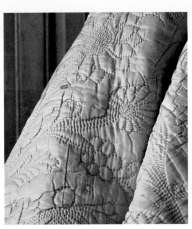

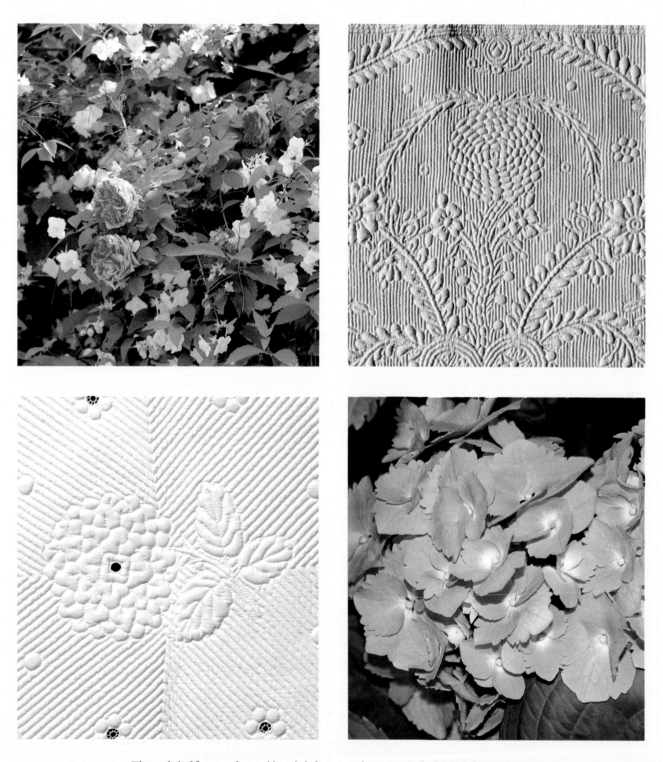

The symbol of flowers refers to old symbols from several centuries, indeed several thousand years.
The rose is the flower of pure love, the iris, the emblem of royalty.

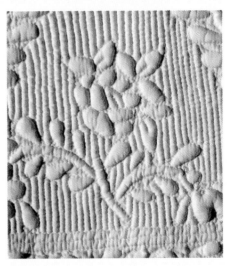

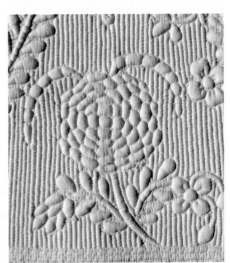
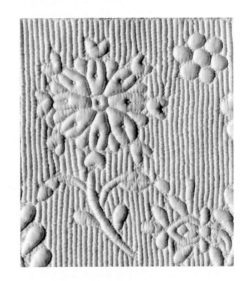

The thistle, cornflower, cornpoppy, marguerite, holly (butcher broom) and wild flowers in general, as well as plants with tinctural and medicinal qualities, that women assembled in bouquets, used in tisanes, served as models to the country 'boutis' and made sumptuous 'boutis' for the towns.

Harvests in large bouquets.

Fruits

Bunch of grapes + leaves . . . . C, V.
(round grapes = chasselas, oval grapes = Muscat)
Pears + leaves + flowers . . . . V.
Apricots + leaves + flowers . . . . V, J.
Burst pomegranates . . . . V.
Whole pomegranates . . . . V, J.
Pomegranates cut in two . . . . V, J.
Whole melons . . . . V.
Melons cut in two . . . . V.
Acorns + leaves . . . . V, P.
Acorns by themselves . . . . V, P.
Figs . . . . V.
Nuts . . . . V.
Pineapple + leaves (1733) . . . . V.
Almonds . . . . J.
Large Almonds . . . . J.

*Fruit cut open
with its seeds.*

*Fruit cut in two,
showing the nut or an
almond in the centre.*

Objects

Key . . . . J.
Lyre . . . . V.
Quarter of a fan . . . . V.
Quarter of the sun . . . . C, V.
Flaming torches, crossed . . . . C.

Leaves

Rosemary .... V.	Laurel leaves .... V.
Leaves from the Olive tree ..... V.	Indeterminate leaves .... V, J.
Acanthus leaves .... V, P.	Thorny Acanthus leaves .... V, J.
Branches and tendrils	Palm leaves .... V.
from the vines .... V, J.	Palmette .... V.
Oak leaves .... V, P.	Single oak leaves .... V, P.
	Cypres .... V.

Other motifs

Scallop shells .... J.	Other shells .... V.
Protestant Dove .... J.	Ribbon and Bow .... V.
Maltese Cross .... V.	Coats of Arms .... V.

The cypress is a sign that identifies with the Midi. It is used here as a symbol of a region; its silhouette is impregnated in the memory of the women. On the 'boutis', it is not a sign of mourning, as it was done for happy days. The pine tree is a symbol of immortality; the cypress, frequent in the Mediterranean is part of a spontaneous iconography.

Vegetables

Artichokes + leaves .... V.	Pepper .... V.
Pea-pod + flower	Little tomatoes + leaves .... V.
or the fruit of the acacia(?) .... J.	

Containers

Baskets of all forms	
(handles are rare) .... V, J.	Baskets (flowers) .... V.
Antique Vases .... V.	Medici Vases .... V, J.
Base (motif used on wallpaper) . V.	Jars (Anduze style) .... J.
Sea shell .... V.	Cornucopias .... V.
Urns* .... V, C, J.	Suggestions of Cornucopias ...... V.
Little Pictures* .... V, C, J.	The cauldron from the chimney .. V, J.
Medallions* .... V, J.	'Cassolette'*
Signs* .... V, C, J.	(small earthenware dish) .... V, J.
Hearts .... V, J.	
*small motifs	

In the second half of the 19th century, women threw, onto the last 'boutis', the vegetables from their garden, healing flowers and wild flowers.

A basket that is often shown: if its form has hardly evolved, the bouquet on certain 'vanes' has been modified.

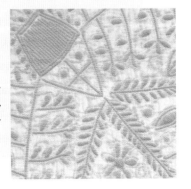

Compositions

Cornucopias with flowers . . . . V.
Arranged flowers in vases or baskets . . . . C, V, J.
Branch with fruits + tree flowers + leaves . . . . V, J.
Branch with fruits + leaves . . . . V, J.
Cups (with feet) garnished with fruits . . . . V.
Cups (with feet) garnished with fruits and flowers . . . . V.
Branch with flowers, buttons, wilting flowers and fruits J.
Initials in a medallion (big or small) . . . . V, J.
Wedding date in a little medallion or near a border . . . . V, J.

The people are placed in view on one side and the other of the central square. Are they speaking to one another? Their position, in comparison with the ensemble, has been carefully chosen.

Ornamental motifs

Wreaths . . . . V.
Scrolls . . . . V.
Louis XVI pearl necklaces . . . . V.
Single pearls . . . . V.
Festoons with a large internal decoration . . . . V.
Plumes . . . .
Branches, boughs, leafy arabesques . . . . V, C, J.
Undulating garland of leaves . . . . V, C, J.
Garland of leaves in broken lines . . . . V, C, J.
Undulating garland of leaves, or in broken lines
running over large surfaces . . . . V.
Borders with repeating motifs, symbols of prosperity . . V, J.
Borders with different motifs . . . . J.

The acanthus leaf was inspired from antique models, and has been combined with other decoration. It is frequent in architecture.

Harvests

Maize with leaves . . . . J.
Wheat with leaves . . . . C, V.
Bunches of grapes with leaves . . . . V.
An arbour with bunches of grapes
mixed with flowers . . . . V.
Little pears (grown on a cordon)
from Saint Jean . . . . V.
Certain fruits . . . . V.

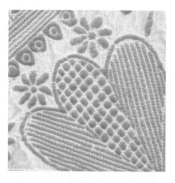

Maize is represented in three parts. The ear at the centre, and on each side there are large leaves.

The sheaf symbolises wealth and extravagance of gifts. It is a perpetual offering.

Hearts

Single heart . . . . J.

Passionate heart . . . . C, J.

Heart pierced with an arrow . . . V, J.

Intertwining hearts . . . . V.

Hearts used as containers
for bouquets . . . . V, J.

Beasts

Standing dog . . . . V.

Sitting dog . . . . V.

Cock . . . . V.

Pair of birds: facing one another . . . C, V.

Bees . . . . V.

huddled one against the other . . . . C.

Birds . . . . V, P.

wings open (male bird) . . . . C.

Doves or Pigeons . . . . C, V.

A pair of eagles, embracing . . . . V.

Parrots . . . . V.

Phoenix . . . . V.

Single Eagle . . . . V.

Lions . . . . V.

Peacock . . . . V.

Single Bird . . . . V, C, J.

Architecture

A mill . . . . V.

Little temple on a hillock . . . . V.

Mound/pile of stones . . . . V.

Canopy . . . . V.

People

Woman standing with right arm raised (frontal) . . . . V.

Man sat with a bird (profile) . . . . V.

Roman soldier + sitting dog (frontal) . . . . V.

Seated woman with a distaff (profile) . . . . V.

The people are silhouetted in a field of vegetation, where the antiquity gives to the whole piece, an imposing solemnity. The woman is raising her hand and is speaking, whilst the man is taming a bird.

Geometric motifs

Square divided into little squares (9, 16, 49! 81!) . . . . V.

Stars of 5, 6 or 8 points . . . . V.

Lozenges divided into little lozenges . . . . J.

Lozenges boxed on inside another . . . . J.

Lozenges with internal divisions or an enclosed flower . . . J.

Background motifs

No motif (in this case, there is a field covered in vegetation) . . . . V.

Vermicelli* in lozenges . . . . C, V.

Vermicelli in stars . . . . C, V.

Vermicelli following a straight thread . . . . V, J, P.

Alternating vermicelli (on the bias and also following the warp) . . . . C, V.

Vermicelli on the bias . . . . P, J.

Vermicelli of different widths (from 2mm to 7-8mm!) . . . . V.

(wider and wider in the mountain regions and on the big 'vanes'.)

Vermicelli in a "mistralade" (curved, going in all directions) . . . . C, V.

No rule, i.e. the vermicelli are in straight lines, in all directions

Square paving (sides of 2cm or less) . . . . V, J.

Lozenge paving (sides of 1cm or less) . . . . J.

Vermicelli in arcs, forming shells . . . . V.

(possibly inspired by the mounds of Indian trees of life)

*Vermicelli – small channel bordered by two lines
of stitches in which a tuft of cotton is placed.

Tools

Tools used for the harvest . . . . V.
Rake
Sickle / Scythe
Flail

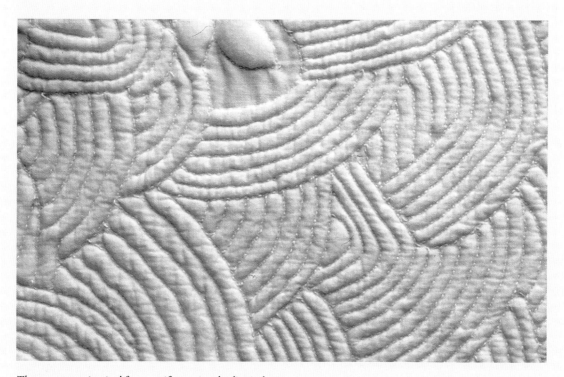

These curves are inspired from motifs on printed calico in layers.

The secret language of the bridal 'jupon'

What a wonderful language is that of the bridal 'jupon', the language of love, and a secret language from the dawn of time! Some of these flowering borders have kept their mystery for a so long, because, even with a few pointers to help us decipher what we could call a code, the transcription is both difficult and hazardous to the uninitiated eyes. The story is beautiful! It is the breathing of the plants (those of the 16th century are perhaps there for a reason), which has dictated the ballet of wedding flowers. Nature, in harmony with man's life, offers all its generous promises.

The flower comes in a variety of forms: budding, half-open, almost open and then blooming. Its petals fall. As to the fruit, it is recognisable from its shape, presenting several cuts, showing the pulp and the seeds. We have complicated it further by suggesting that there are two plants on the same branch. Clusters of holly and single berries detached for the butchers broom, a bunch of grapes or the pomegranate flower. The leaves of these plants appear on the same branch, proving from it that there are several possible explanations.

The stalks complicate the stuffing, as do some other unexpected elements – sepals, pistils and stamens – removed from their correct location and lost in other areas; we are in a picture madness which goes well with the passion of love.

The girl, with both her creative and her daring side, enters into and bonds with this creation, which she hijacks to her profit. Designs, for which she does not always know the true significance - the point of the thorn and the burr - are altered with tenderness in order to soften them, adding her personal touch a little here and there.

But where are the roots?
But where are the seeds?
Where is the running water?

Illustration of holly and butchers broom on the same branch

Writing of women

A little stitch or a little bit of thread was enough to underline the natural indent on a piece of fruit (apricot, plum and the biggest vein on a leaf). A little stitch was sufficient to divide areas of different colours (borders and nuances on petals).

A little stitch… a little bit of thread… it's nothing as we say, but it is part of a tree of life written on our country 'vanes' worked in large vermicelli. Work of art or of imagination, it is sewn into a maze of vanishing branches…

Little, little stitches… a little bit of thread… it is nothing, but they are the love hearts that are blooming in the light of life…

Little stitches… a little bit of thread… a tuft of cotton… It is an anonymous page of love forgotten in the silence of the armoires.

It's nothing…
Where are the seeds?
Where are the roots?
Where is the running water?
A little stitch, a little bit of thread, everything has a meaning…
But… where is the running water?
Where are the seeds?

For the embroidery of the interior, the 'tour de force' of the designers was to give perspective where there wasn't any. Thanks to the technique, where there are only two dimensions as the piece is flat, the third is created by volume.

In a general sense, it is the form which was privileged, that is to say, the outline, as the shape of each component is well represented with a refined line, removing unnecessary details: leaves that are too detailed or complicated are stylised in order to appreciate the contour.

Two main plans come out of the piece:
– The view from above
– The perfect profile

When the flowers and the leaves are closely interwoven – even touching – they are perfectly defined and do not cut one into the other, as is the case in embroidery. The meaning of the design is not the same. One shape, or one part "has not been eaten" to the profit of another; each flower was studied one by one.

Saint Aubin wrote, "The design is the basis…, the foundation of the embroidery, it determines the shape, the beautiful distribution; it brings harmony, regulates the proportions, adds new merit to the work… the design is the soul of the embroidery." The volume has replaced the role played by colour. This first representation is similar to stone sculptures that embellish the lower friezes of cathedrals and the column capitals of temples and churches; besides, embroidery

FLORA AND VEGETATION ON THE 'BOUTIS'

The barbs that coat the corn are not shown by the stitching…

as long as it is not another cereal… or lavander.

The vein on the leaf is shown as it is an integral part of the element.

A piece of down, a hair in real life.

A fine element in reality gives volume to the 'boutis'.

A larger element in reality gives a more important volume. It is intentionally exaggerated.

But where are the seeds, where is the water?

'emboutie' has been classed since the 13th century in the group of raised embroidery.

The flowers created by the painters of the 18th and 19th centuries were brought closer together in the second "naturalist" trend. It married the floral art, which had blossomed in the Alsacien printed calicos. Some perspective effects can be found, as well as more precise details: stamens and pistils. These elements are in the correct place in their motif on the 'boutis'.

Finally, the botanical spirit breathed in this textile language. The accumulation of elements belonging to the same plant underlines the ease of identification. The progression is visible:
– The single flower,
– The flower on its stalk, or on a branch,
– The flower, its leaf or leaves,
– The fruit, its flowers and its leaves.

These representations are current with orchard fruits, Provencal fruits for preference, of a small size.

The stitching technique is closely related to the shape, and vice-versa. Nothing was done at random. Each surface was considered in conjunction with another. The chosen motifs were not only in harmony with the size of the piece to be 'boutisser' and with the style of border and the choice of centre, but also in relation to the future use of the piece ('vane' and 'pétasson' did not have the same purpose), as a badly mastered technique led to the material being deformed. Following mistakes, a level surface could be covered with waves that could not be corrected.

Large pieces ('vanes', 'vanons' and 'coussinières') were composed not only for aesthetic reasons, but also technical reasons. Their compositions have certain similarities to those of shawls, scarves and carpets.

To find solutions to all this information, a team developed the project. It was made up of a designer or an artist, a set designer and the master of the piece, in charge of the technique.

FLOWERS AND 'BOUTIS'

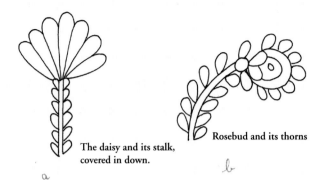

The daisy and its stalk, covered in down.

Rosebud and its thorns

a

b

c

A primrose in 'boutis'.

FLOWERS IN ALL STAGES

A flower in profil.

A marigold seen from above.

Flowers and their stamens.

Flower and seeds.

A petal.

Spirit in which the 'boutis' is to be done.

a

Identical elements.

All the elements from the same plant or flower have served the birth of a new branch.

b.

Symbols of forever

Since the dawn of mankind, man has left reminders of his life on cave walls[7]. They drew hunting scenes with precision and hinted at perspective, with details of movement, using the wall and its relief to carefully depict an environment rich with emotions.

Later, potteries, rugs and modest everyday objects were to be decorated portraying the identity of their milieu…

In the gardens of Tuthmosis, the little princess gathered armfuls of scented flowers and chose the most beautiful fruits bursting with sunshine. On the long flat-bottomed little boat she glided into the Nile Valley and left her offerings in the sacred temple. Using pictures, the scribe wrote of these rituals that have been lost in the mists of time. In other places, and on other continents, other men, without knowing it, used the same mysterious symbols, creating similar pieces. These identical obsessions led them to mark the fabrics that were worn during certain ceremonies. On the cloth that was reserved for the highest dignitaries, they drew their history, choosing symbols personal to them.

Our symbols are sometimes different as they are written in an Indo-European culture. We use them in many mediums sometimes giving them other meanings.

Fabrics charged with meaning

Since the 16th century, on the 'courtepointes' of the Royal house and those of the Princes, the embroideries in 'piqûres de Marseille' moved away from floral art – which was already heavily charged with meaning – thanks to the coats of arms or embroidered heraldry. A whole symbolism that not only translates the taste of the time, the refinement of a higher social class, but also permitted reference points with regards to identification, as well as an approximate date.

On later works, every motif that was different from the plant context was to have the value of a symbol. Now, what is a symbol? It is an illustration to which we attach a meaning. An object or an animal could represent a power, a belief (a classic example is the heart, the symbol of love).

The symbol's place is on the surface is not down to chance. Whatever the created work of art is, it is chosen and thought through. On the 'courtepointes' embroidered by 'boutis', the best places are in the corners of the centre, on the median lines. The symbol, melted into the background, or conspicuous in a medallion would not have the same meaning. Coptic fabrics[8] discovered in the excavations of Antinoe in Upper Egypt are the proof of a researched composition and a placing of the motifs according to their importance. In

The temple represents the sacred city between heaven and earth.
The centre of the world is always represented by a building,
(for example, the temple of Solomon.)

Vanon from the end of the 19th century, initialled L.B. The initials are
the symbols of identity, preciously closed in little medallions,
beautifully compacted.

antique art, the same rules were observed. Carpets from Central Europe were carefully arranged, with the motivations of keeping undesirables – animals and insects – out of the house or tent.

Accompanied by other elements spread across textiles, the symbols speak and complement each other, signing the story which evokes not only the life of the women, but also that of the men.

From where does one approach this choreography of shapes, and how to tackle all these generous sentiments without damaging them?

An earth full of promises

The vegetable world in its totality, with its bowl of plenty, have let the flowers and the fruits escape, evoking the fertility of the nourishing earth, calling to the gods to spill forth their good-will onto the young couple. On the 'boutis', the harvests and the pickings are both present, and one must know how to read between the lines, to the work in the fields and the organisation of farming activities; however, the mixture of forms does not suggest one particular season.

The wheat sheaf, several or one at a time, symbolises the harvest, abundance and prosperity, and also the profusion of life.

Excavations have shown that wheat was present in 6000BC, near Martigues. It was grown at Salernes in the Var 4700BC just as it was in Nîmes. Thousands of years old, it was a symbol represented with precision in the Valley of the Kings in Egypt.

In the plant collection, flowers and leaves share a love story that is as old as the hills, with man. The flower, symbol of love and harmony, returns us to the Garden of Eden to find childhood purity. Widely used in ancient civilisations and in medieval roman art, acanthus wreaths hem the capitals of columns and the lower friezes on churches.

The iris in a stylised form is represented from the 3rd millennium BC on the thrones of the Egyptian pharaohs, and was taken to signify royalty, as long as it is not the lily, as these two flowers argue over being the origin of the royal emblem. The peony, from China, breathes richness and honour. The rosette shows every flower of the daisy family. We recognise it from its central dial bordered with a variable number of petals and sepals. The flowers and florets represented since the beginning of history and art explain the divine as well as fertility.

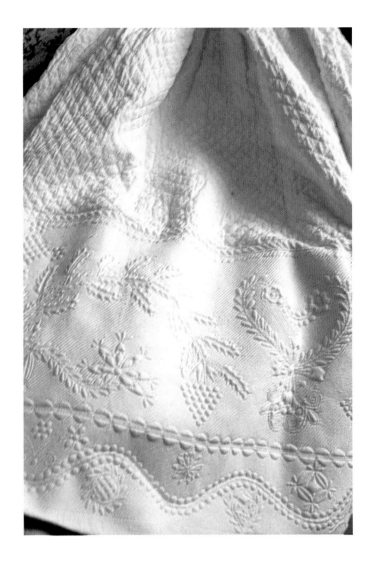

The vegetable world, with its foliage and flowers, evoking fertility.

Flowers and leaves share with man
a history as old as the world.

The size of the divine

Preferred theme throughout the decorative arts, the divine expresses itself on every continent and touches every religion. The vine and the climbing vine appear among the trees of life in Paradise, and wine, drink of the gods, invites us to immortality. Equally, other trees lead us towards esoteric values: the olive tree as a sign of peace, and the laurel singing of glory.

Branches of ivy weaving a garland on the marriage 'courtepointe' have previously rippled on the dresses of Egyptian dancers and musicians as well as on Byzantine ceramics. In Roman and Merovingian art, ivy was associated with the leaf of the vine, and of the acanthus. They were sculpted in medieval art. It was magnificently present in all religious architecture. Symbols of eternal life, the ivy and pinecones give sense for the less enigmatic.

Since the first Christian art, the palmette was to replace the palm tree, which symbolises life, and to complete the consecration the sun and its beneficial rays showered the earth with cosmic influences.

Our trees of life in bouquets plunge their roots into the vases or baskets holding the fertile earth containing the seeds. The opposite of the Chinese or Indian trees, ours are neither inhabited by strange animals, as is the case on Coptic fabrics[9] or even the Indian palempores[10], nor by people accompanying the arabesques of wallpaper, as was the fashion under Louis XIV.

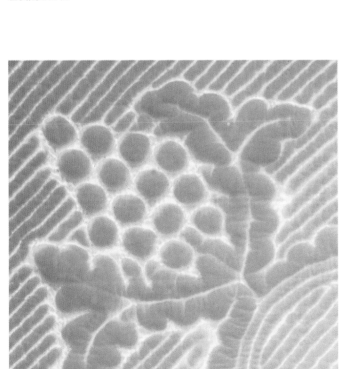

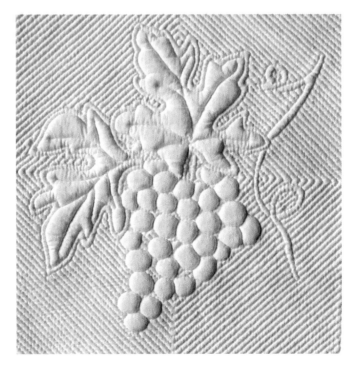

The vine is a sacred tree, the wine is a drink of the gods. It is the figure of the tree of life, of immortality.

Between heaven and earth

That the celebration be the best possible, some animal figures have appeared brightening up the 'vanes' and the 'pétassons', creating a feast for the eyes. The birds, in this vein, have a choice place. Alone or in pairs – facing one another or snuggled up one against the other – they suggest a whole range of sentiments. Happiness is symbolised by a pair of phoenix, fidelity by a pair of turtledoves, but, whatever the chosen variety, felicitations accompanied the young couple.

With its magnificent plumage, the peacock represents pride and one's appearance. The chimera represents a disproportionately large imagination or even a weak or tyrannical sovereign.

The dog, associated with warriors by the Celts, has always been considered as a guide in man's life.

Certain birds, like the phoenix or the peacock, were compared with immortality. In the past, in the Nile Valley the phoenix was considered a magical bird. When it appeared at dawn, its flamboyant red plumage dazzled the whole region. Disappearing into the darkness to rise again from the ashes, the phoenix announced the beneficial floods of the Nile. Little messengers from beyond, all birds are the bonds between heaven and earth.

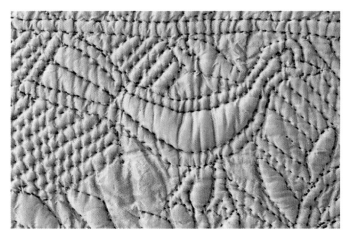

Birds are the little messengers between heaven and earth.
Pigeons and doves symbolise faithful love, often shown in pairs.
The peacock symbolises immortality, the phoenix resurrection.

Refined constructions

The geometric forms that appear on certain 'boutis' from the end of the 18th century merit some of our attention. Circles, lozenges, triangles and squares were represented with random frequency.

Circles in a perfect form symbolise the cosmic sky, but can also represent a magic line that is not to be crossed. Both the sun and gold are drawn as circles. Maybe created by spontaneous gestures, many coiling motifs sprinkled here and there on the country 'boutis' imprison the sunlight in its spiralling movements.

Squares are almost always present, divided up into a multitude of little squares, of which the number varies. They are often found side by side with rosettes, whose numbers of petals differ from one 'boutis' to the next. They serve as departure points for leafy branches, and are sometimes written into the circle, symbol of the sun. The repetition of the motifs, these in particular, announce fertility. If the square brings to mind a world of secrets, but also represents nature, then it is also the symbol of the world.

The triangle is also known as fertility. When the point is aimed towards the top, it could suggest the rise of creation. With its three sides, it is related to the sky. Two triangles together form the Star of David: one representing the earth and the other the sky. In the same way, in the lozenge a combination of the divine and the earthly are found, as long as it is not an expression of femininity.

Stars of 4, 5, 6 and 8 points are represented. Certain ones make us think of flamboyant stars used in masonry, but their festooned sides are perhaps only a sought-after ornament.

It is, however, interesting to know that the five pointed flamboyant star shows man standing. It represents wisdom. Other stars as sources of light have a relationship with the symbolism of numbers, depending on the number of points.

The cross is not a frequent symbol. As an old solar symbol it was found in the excavations of Troy in Syria, and became one of the essential shapes of the medieval Church, where time, space, earth and sky meet. It indicates the four Cardinal points, the basis of our compass points: terrestrial, spatial, celestial and temporal.

Stars refer to the divine.

119

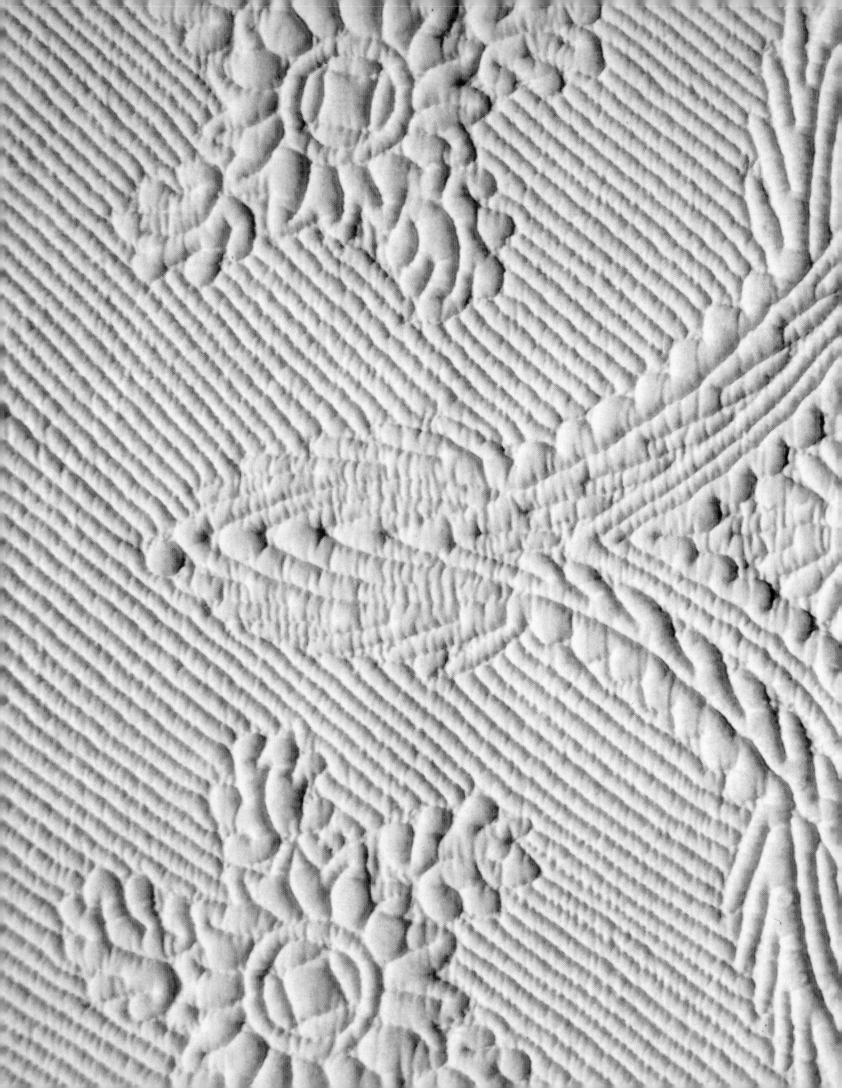

Mysterious squares

Strange squares are sprinkled with insistence over the surface of the 'boutis'. Looking at the collection and the comments that flow from them, we could say that the square is represented time and time again. While circles exist in a natural state in our world, this motif is geometrical, created completely by the hand of man. Its surface is noticeable at first glance, as it is often compartmentalized in a mass of little squares of which the number varies, and can even go as high as 81!

These geometric forms are found mainly in combination with flowers. The number of petals on these flowers is unvarying on the same piece of work, but different on another; it often relates to the daisy family or simply a 'flower' in general. The repetition 'to infinity' of alternating squares and flowers gives rise to a flowering field; sometimes these same motifs are found stuck to leafy branches or serving as vases or as containers giving birth to vegetation.

When placed on certain 'vanes', the squares appear somewhat isolated, often along the middle lines and in the corners disturbing the harmony created by the curving foliage and the bouquets; in these cases, their incongruous presence only accentuates the importance of their symbolism which is difficult to decipher. Numerous squares on one piece are found at the very end of the 18th century, that is to say a little after abandoning the improvement of stitches by the factories of Marseilles and the region. The art of the 'boutis' was taken up by women, who were to take over and enhance, in turn, their finery whose beauty dazzled the daily scene.

Like the palindromes of the Middle Ages who showed the secret sites to only the initiated who would be able to interpret them, there is no doubt that these squares are inevitably important. Certain ones are bedecked, in the four corners, with petals or with leaves in little clusters, which should be translated by "this motif belongs to the plant world".

In the representation, which goes back to the dawn of time, only the square symbolises nature and the earth. The vertical line is the fertile one, whilst the horizontal line represents the passive form of femininity. Adding this all together leads us to conclude that the square pattern represents seeds.

At the beginning of this analysis there were two facts: the smallest feature has some significance, as does the smallest of stitches. At the beginning of the female chain, certain women have proved their precision by not missing a single detail. Then, over the passage of time, other women have reproduced the designs because they were pretty… and then ruined a few through bad copying.

By extending the same thought, vases, baskets, cauldrons and other geometric forms, bordered or not by plant forms, serve as an anchor point for trees of life in bouquets, symbolising the earth, fertilised by the seeds.

The square pattern represents the seeds, and they are preciously preserved in their enclosed motifs.

An identical square pattern is found in other containers (vases and baskets). It is sometimes surrounded on the four corners by petal motifs (just like a lozenge for that matter). These signs define its belonging to the plant world. This representation exists along the length of the flower stalks (thorns and hairs) and was used to embellish many motifs bordering the frieze, which rises and falls along the length of the 'jupon'. These borders are enriched with seeds or signs that relate to vegetation. It is in these stalks that water and sap are found, or in little dewdrops in the form of pearls that cover the surface of certain 'boutis'.

The roots, rare or difficult to recognise, are underneath the base of the basket: it is exceptional to see this representation. Later, the roots were moved, reproduced elsewhere several times out of context, losing their significance. It is in this way that from hand-to-hand, drawing after drawing, several plant elements have been recreated, making a new beauty from a new nature. Each element is represented, but is no longer in its place; the stamens burst forth from a crown that surrounds the flowers, the sepals appear under the petals and recreate, in their turn, other flowers. It is a total upheaval of the plant world, revised and corrected by the hands of women.

The symbol of seeds.

122

Hearts... and love

On the bridal 'jupon' and on the 'vanes', cascades of flowering branches flow out of precious hearts like little jewels. These hearts are particular as they are worked and sculpted into a much sought-after shape, winding up in a crosier of ferns. The raised part of the fabric has carved the interior surface into a criss-cross; while at the edge, the shorter or longer threads lead towards the base, decorating this traditional symbol of love.

At this stage, passion must be put aside, giving way to reason. There are two sorts of hearts. Those that are well defined, with a neat border that can also be intertwined, and the others, in which we find the seeds that we already identified in the squares. To put the accent on this stunning discovery, and to confirm this hypothesis, little flowers are present inside these hearts. They are waiting to grow... They are the future flowers, whose roots are the bulbs.

The heart and love.

So, all hearts are not about love! Who would have believed it?

These are bulbs that have their roots in the tightly curled floating hair that belongs to an angel. These hearts are just as precious as the love hearts, as they are the symbol of fertility, of life, and of life to come. The purity of their shape is created from a fine aesthetic quality because they are simply so beautiful, and, because in the eyes of those that chose them, they were the symbols of love.

In the west, the heart is associated with the spirit. It is the base of sentiment. It is the symbol of love, par excellence.

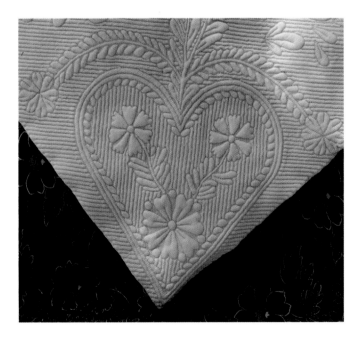

123

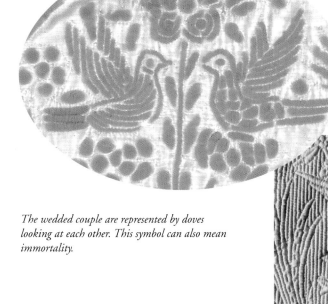

The wisdom of women

Religion was not represented by particularly distinctive signs, but hinted at through the delicacy of the flowers and the following symbols: the Lily and the Acanthus leaves for the Catholic religion; the scallop shell was used by pilgrims, and was found engraved or sculpted on the priories. If the Protestants had sometimes opted for more sobriety in their designs, composition, or in the dove, it is no less beautiful. On each side of the Rhone, the 'boutis' was embroidered, passionately created by women who were mastering the same gestures, living through the same events that accompany the different ages of life.

Each one respected her part in a stream of thought, but it was love that each one of them expressed in their own way. In expressing in their works of art their hopes for life, they became one through the eternal language of the troubadours.

Sung by all the poets, the rosebud or the opened rose remained the flower of love. Its perfume and beauty is associated with the representation of this passionate sentiment. On the bridal 'jupon' the language of Cupid is written in letters of roses and messages of flowers. It breathes in sculpted generous hearts and balances itself on flowering boughs. The harmonious curves suggest happiness whilst the bulbous hearts, the receptacles of life, foretell the joyous signs of the future.

The loving couple, or true love, is represented by birds, pigeons, doves or eagles entwined with lit torches, finding its consecration in this glorious celebration.

The scallop shell is a Catholic symbol. It adorns the pediments of priories, constructed along the length of the four paths which led the pilgrims to Saint-Jacques of Compostella. The southern path passed via Arles and St Gilles. These were carried as a known emblem. They are found on 'vanes' as are other emblems of the same type.

Two pigeons love each other with a tender love... remarkable 'boutis' from 1861.

The wedded couple are represented by doves looking at each other. This symbol can also mean immortality.

Grannies, grannies

In the beautiful countryside of the Languedoc, where the protestant tradition is still strong, it is important to note that the Huguenot cross did not leave its mark on the works and celebratory clothes which are part of the divine.

On the beautiful earth of Provence, the Catholics discreetly flaunted their religion: on the other hand, the presence of an ensemble of symbols – always the same – on certain 'vanes', enclosed an area bordered by the Rhone (bowl of flowers, scallop shell, a heart with a star on top, a pair of birds, a lyre…). Nuptial 'courtepointes', bridal 'jupons', birth 'pétassons' used for ceremonies representing the different ages of life are still adorned with secret motifs which will whisper to each other for a long time yet in the warmth of the slightly open armoires.

The coats-of-arms of the 16th and the 17th centuries belonging to the higher ranked 'houses' have become over the years the monograms and figures showing the identity or the alliance of families by marriage. Whilst the traditions of bull-fighting punctuate the order of a festive calendar in harmony with the seasons of the 'bovine'[11] so dear to the Marquis de Baroncelli and to the whole population around the Rhone delta, the 'bouvine' did not leave its footprint on the 'boutis' or on our precious household finery.

The cicada, the olives, the herdsman's house, the farm-houses and the animals of our region are absent.

The cauldron, of which the content brings to mind the hearth, represents a feminine activity, but the work in the field is hardly evoked. A 'courtepointe' on which appears a sheaf as well as the tools accompanying the harvest (the rake, the sickle, the flail…) shows a male achievement. The guild signs – set square and compass – so frequent in architecture are equally absent. This inventory of missing motifs, juxtaposed with an inventory of visible motifs and symbols allows us to enlarge the field of thought as to the existing illustrations, but also on the levels of implementation seen thus far.

As from the collections studied, three levels of creation come to light. When the professional workshops of the Marseilles region as well as others began to decline towards the end of the 18th century, other more modest places of knowledge took up the technique of unbridled success, which required a rigorous apprenticeship and constant practice. The second level, a different repertoire from the first but just as interesting, fulfilled the domestic needs and followed the current philosophies bringing beautiful things into the home. In their turn, the women's hands preserved this knowledge until the middle of the 19th century. Industrialisation and economic upheaval came to change the way of living and thinking of a whole region. "Hand-made" was replaced by "machine-made". Like Beauty sleeping in the wood, the 'boutis', just like a phoenix was to sleep for a little more than a century before it rose from its ashes.

NOTES

1. Motifs of stylised flowers on good quality printed calicoes.
2. Manufacturer of wallpaper.
3. Calico printer (toiles de Jouy).
4. Arabesques: certain embellishments made up of plants, branches and coils, which could constitute an assembly of objects bringing to mind pleasant ideas.
5. See the catalogue of the Bordeaux exhibition, 1998, *La route des Indes*.
6. Map and chronology of the journey of printed calico in Europe. Taken from the map shown at the 'Musée de l'impression sur étoffe', Mulhouse.
7. Grottes de Lascaux; caves discovered by Abbot Breuil and Léon Laval in 1940.
8. See *La route des Indes*, 1998, catalogue of the Bordeaux exhibition.
9. Ibid.
10. See *Circulades Languedociennes de l'an mille*, Krzysztof Pawlowski.
11. The name given to all of the traditions linked to the bull in the Camargue (festivals, games, races, life and work).

Lit torches and quivers represent ardent love.
The lyre is a symbol of harmony.

A decorative art saved from oblivion

From Catherine to Mira

"Catherine de Medicis[1] spent her evenings toiling away on her silk compositions" and Madame de Maintenon[2], fascinated by embroidery and attentive to the affairs of the kingdom, performed her work diligently in silence, whilst King Louis XIV held council; her passion was such that she even embroidered during coach journeys.

Embroidery reached its peak of splendour during the 16th and 17th centuries. Since 1292, embroiderers and their ecclesiastical counterparts had been organised into establishments, then into brotherhoods from 1471. The art of embroidery was taught in a workshop where the Master, surrounded by several fellow workers, trained two apprentices. Following the guild principal, the completion of the masterpiece completed the apprenticeship and gave access to the trade. The most gifted of embroiderers were part of the Royal household and were more highly rewarded.

In 1686, a certain Lherminot, embroider to the King, received 650 livres per annum, whilst another embroiderer called Baland, embroiderer to the Gobelins, received only 150.

Contrary to popular belief, women were not excluded from the profession. Members of the female religious communities entered into the ranks of the professionals. Madame de Montespan and Madame de Maintenon created embroidery workshops in the convents. They taught needlework to the young girls of the poorer nobility and, in the provinces, the same organisation was put in place.

Embroidery Kit in heavy ivory, with its 'boutis' needle.

The embroiderers only showed distain for ordinary work.

The art of embroidery

The embroidery workshops were situated around the furniture manufacturers, close to the cotton or silk fabric producers. It is due to this that for the production of a 'courtepointe' in 'piqûres de Marseille' or in 'broderie emboutie', the client gave his order either directly to the manufacturer, or to a merchant. It was the custom of the time to deal with every stage of a product, from the choice of the fabric, its colour and the dimensions, right up to the stitching. The merchant-makers also had the same approach. The workshop and workforce were linked in production, even when they were several kilometres away, under the direction of a Master-embroiderer or Mistress. Several convents had their own workshops authorised to practise spinning, weaving and embroidery. Some were of higher reputation than others. The young girls of the poorer nobility and the orphans benefited from a general and artistic schooling during which their needlework was perfected. The income received from the sale of their work went towards their board and lodging.

The three categories of workshop from which the 'broderie emboutie' could be taught and practised until the 19th century were:
– Professional workshops, with specialists earning between 30 to 40 sols per day,
– Parallel workshops attached to the teaching places of the young noble girls,
– Convents that were developing, for their own use, a commercial circuit.

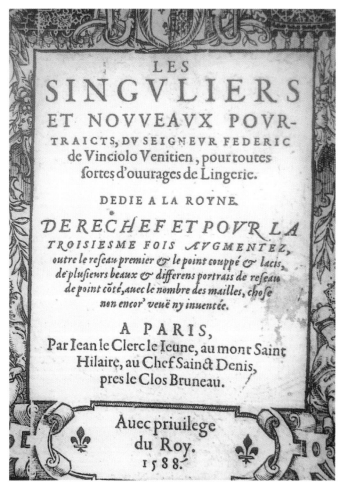

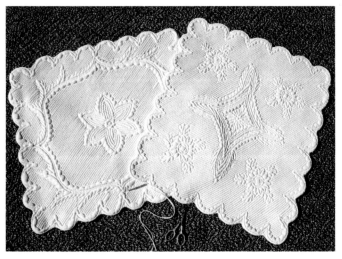

'Pétassons' from Provence.
The centres with chiselled stars impose their relief in lumps.

The professional embroiderers were disdainful of ordinary pieces. Therefore in their workshops they undertook embroidery for Church ornaments, the furniture[3] and beds[4] of noble families, and a few pieces for particular people. Other workshops produced more ordinary pieces and were under the leadership of the upholsterer and the 'futainiers'.[5]

"The drawing is the soul of embroidery", said Saint-Aubin. The embroiderers, with good reason, called in artists who were well known for quality designs. The queens welcomed foreign painters to the court, Italians in particular. Catherine de Medici invited the Venetian Frédérico Vinciolo in 1587. He published in Paris a collection of designs that had been a huge success. But he was not the first to do this. A Florentine beat him to it: in 1530, Francesco Pellegrino brought out *'La Fleur de la science de pourtraicture et patrons de broderie'*, with motifs taken from an oriental collection including fabrics and ceramics, everything that was from the origins of trade in the Mediterranean.

The sources of inspiration were inexhaustible. The queens introduced embroidery frames, their linen chests overflowing with squares of fine fabrics and gauzes that had been drawn on.

129

Embroidery "en ronde-bosse" on the 'boutis'

"The work 'en bosse' could only be the work of professionals."[6]

The love and passion for raised design gave rise to distinctive and skilful techniques using a quantity of materials, sometimes precious in order to fashion the surface of a fabric originally smooth and flat. "The noble and gentle art of needlework"[7] judiciously uses cords, pearls, 'paillons'[8], 'aventurine',[9] metal plaques, a large variety of purl points, 'cartisane',[10] all sorts of tricks in order to sculpt the surface in embroidery. To give volume to the chosen decoration, the arabesques, foliage or flowers, from the exterior or the interior, the embroiderer determines the process that will catch the light, play with reflection, and enrich the fabrics. The most gifted made padding with the help of models cut from carton or from cork, which permitted them to raise the embroidery in relation to the base material. The cotton stuffing was also used under the silk to be embroidered. "La broderie eslevée ou enlevée", "la broderie haute" uses the techniques from this group as well as that of raised embroidery, "en bosse", and "en ronde-bosse". Saint Aubin puts 'broderie emboutie' in this category although the volume obtained is due to the quantity of wadding between the two layers of fabric, and not on the surface.

The rare evidence of this specialised technique is scattered in several old books.

Pillowcase embroidered in 'boutis' in all its finery.

The embroidery of the interior

The study made of the collection of 'boutis' shown in this book allow the author to make the following remarks.

'Broderie emboutie' and embroidery on the 'boutis' (known as the real 'boutis') are of the same family. These techniques both require two layers of fabric. The design that is chosen with care is traced onto the first piece. Then the embroiderer puts in the stitches called 'piqué' around each motif, along the length of each of the straight or curved lines, creating the canals, the vermicelli. This is simply known as the stitching, and means that the two pieces of fabric are joined together. Then comes the moment when the piece takes on depth. On the reverse, the embroiderer makes a small hole with a bodkin through one piece of fabric, then gently introduces one of the cotton tufts into one of the motifs with the help of either a boutis needle or a long supple stalk or stem (in this case, the tuft is pushed into the hole), or a bodkin in which case the tuft of cotton must be pulled.

Saint-Aubin, in his book *Art du Brodeur*, was much more miserly with his advice on designs and it would be sensible to bear his wise remarks in mind in the practical section of this book: "To embroider in depth, pictures, ornamental foliage, grotesque figures, fruits or flowers… the embroiderer must have designed on a small frame the different areas of the object, detached one from the other… starting with expressing the largest coverings. Each object therefore has its own fullness of form, totally visible and even a little exaggerated (the work of the most intelligent workers… is often a copy of a model in wax or plaster)."

Mira, Albertine, Julie, Lyse and the others

Mira

On the road that goes from Codognan to Beauvoisin, Mira is working on her boutis. She has stretched her 'couverton' of white cloth on a small frame and she is padding the tufts of cotton into the motifs of her sun of flowers drawn with 'poncifs', with the blue powder still visible. The large carthorse gives a slow lilt to the cart. It is June and the day is going to be hot. Mira is off to visit her family. From nine this morning the cicadas 'casquaillent',[11] time is stretching out in front. Protected by the sun under her wide-brimmed cardboard hat covered in fabric, she carefully watches the cloth swell, breathe and tighten. Her flowers rise and fall breaking out like fireworks on her printed calico skirt. Mira takes advantage of this lost time to pack the pointed leaves.[12] From time to time her brown hand crosses the cloth, caressing it whilst appreciating the density of the stuffing. Her pleasure is intense; her creation leads her through a universe where mediocrity has no place. Between earth and sky, her mind wanders off, evading the everyday thoughts. During the whole journey, she forgets work, which punctuates the journey. A passionate person, the boutis cannot wait.

It takes several hours from Codognan to Beauvoisin. The slow pace of her carthorse will give her the extra time she needs, fiddling here and there to be satisfied with her needlework.

On the banks of the bumpy road, the large chamomiles and poppies are already flowering. Next week, when going to the fields to thin the vines,[13] she needs to remember to pick some cornflowers and some mallow to put in her herb garden, and to draw them when dried. She will be short of cotton to stuff her 'couverton'; her husband needs to think of buying her some skeins in Calvisson at the 'notaire' who is also a trader. Her cousin at Beauvoisin might be able to help out. The 'bonneterie' workshop that she runs in her 'mas' has plenty of stuffing, but everything is weighed; before the bonnet is made, then the bonnets themselves, then the rest of the cotton… It will surely be necessary to go to the market in Nîmes on Monday.

In the pine forest bordering the road, the cicadas' song doubles in strength, the regular clip clop from the horses' hooves gives rhythm to the journey. Without growing weary, with patience solid as a rock, Mira stuffs her 'boutis'. She knows that she will do it again this evening after the meal, as the evening together will be long…

In front of the chimney, the dancing flames, the glow from her oil lamp and the 'veilladou',[14] Mira continues her work of art.

Mira's 'courtepointe'. / The masterpiece of Mira: her 'vane' with its sun of flowers.

131

Albertine

A couple of steps from the Castle at Uzès at Blauzac, in her little house, behind the narrow windows, Albertine embarks on the making of her 'vane de lit'. Her son Félix, now over thirty, has decided to marry and it is time to prepare the wedding presents. She has in her chestnut trunk some beautiful fine cloth from Montpellier and a quantity of skeins of cotton wadding. It's time to choose her favourites from the used 'poncifs' in her collection: the flowers from her garden that she grew with love, bunches of grapes swollen with sugar and little 'boutels'[15] with their tightly packed grapes. She must remember to go to the vines to collect some leaves and draw round the edge onto fabric. Albertine likes sizeable quantities, round pearls like marbles, leaves thick and fleshy…

She chooses a large and generous garland for the centre, and delicate hearts, the symbol of love.

On the large dining room table she places the meticulously ironed cloth, carefully positioning her designs. Afterwards, she rubs it with the chalk stamp, the blue powder rubbing through the pierced surface, and then fixes the designs shown up with the help of an alcohol vaporiser. A final marking with crayon, and she can start her work at last.

Her fine and regular stitching will draw her tirelessly into the small hours, but so what…

Albertine hangs her little 'luns'[16] close by, and from the drawer of her 'verrier'[17] hanging on the wall near the chimney. She has everything in hand. In the drawer of a little piece of furniture, blackened by smoke from oil lamps, her tools are beautifully tidied: bodkins, metal bodkins, 'boutis' needles of all sizes, a collection of thimbles and small scissors. Winter could come! In the little narrow stone-walled streets, in the lea of the wind, or sat near the chimney in the 'rue de Blauzaquet', Albertine savours the promise of happy days to come, surrounded by little ones to love.

In the light of her little 'luns',
Albertine created this wedding 'courtepointe' for her son, Felix.

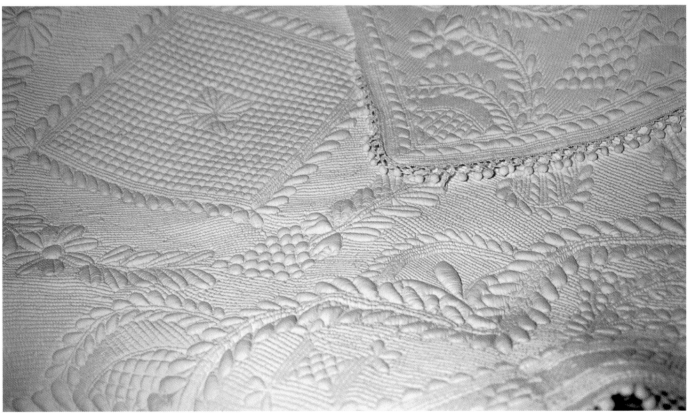

And the others...

Mira's husband is a 'propriétaire' wine grower; Albertine's is of private means. The happy wives who have worn these magnificent 'jupons-frisés' or these 'jupons-jardiniers', with forty to fifty centimetres of 'boutis', grew up in fairly comfortable surroundings and are passionate 'boutisseuses'. At the time of her marriage, Lyse P. wore a beautiful 'jupon' decorated with heavily flowering branches, and as for Julie A., the 'couverton' of a sun of flowers was hers. Both of these women are relatives of Mira, and have the same standard of life.

Originally from Pignan, the family of Madame Greggio has a bridal 'jupon' dating from 1820, with over forty centimetres of 'boutis'. It is a lower middle class family as the grandmother was a peasant, but had money.

All who I questioned talk of mixed farming, which improved their already very comfortable daily life: the chasselas grape, almonds, the wild bay, and the figs. All of them mentioned water and spoke of its importance; the presence of a well, of a little pond, made the daily tasks a little easier, and was a sign of extra wealth.

The superb drawings of Mira, Julie and Lyse belong to the same group and at least prove that in each little country-place there was a workshop with its own way of doing things, its own set of drawings, its own special borders, its embroidery which adds to the whole piece, its specific cloth, its quilting within well-defined dimensions, the same width on the 'jupon' and the same height for the 'boutis'.

Were there two different workshops? Was one dealing with the making of bridal 'jupons' and the other with the 'couvertons', or was there only one workshop?

Exceptional from the outset with their perfect forms balanced, these 'boutis' show the savoir-faire of masters, of people with great artistic experience knowing how to anticipate and visualise the outcome. They are entrusted to the experts' hands, specialised workers who possess a technique adapted to this type of creation. Is it possible, then, that the girls to be married have not made their 'jupon'...? They probably chose the drawings; the decoration could have been changed slightly from one 'jupon' to the next. The initials as well as the date were embroidered to order. In the 17th and 18th centuries, for important made-to-order 'courtepointes', a contract was signed before 'notaire'. In a convent to Saint-Maximin[18], the 'réligieuses' completed the 'boutis' on the bridal 'jupon' – always the same – in "kilometres", and it was the mothers-in-law who offered them to their daughters-in-law!

All of these women, having learnt or practised the 'boutis' at the workshop, have continued the tradition, and put it back into the costume and the trousseau. The savoir-faire has become semi-professional to learn, passed on from mother to daughter, from neighbour to neighbour, spinning its spider's web in the town and country. The drawings from the workshops have probably been retrieved, but have remained in the same area. The women have recreated their 'boutis'; the cloth has become a means of expression, a creation in its entirety. The popular art of the 'boutis' has served as a medium, which has been transformed into a page of writing.

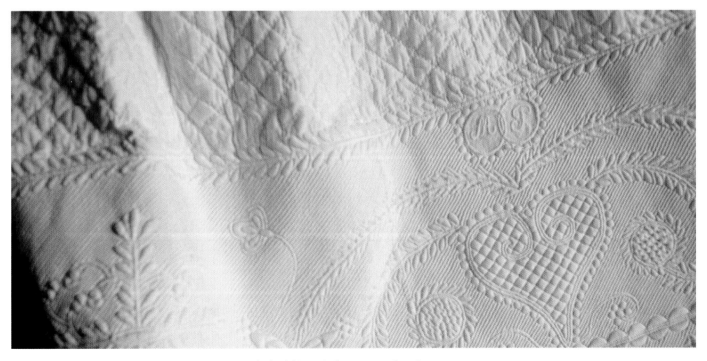

The bridal 'jupon' of Marie P..., from Beauvoisin.

Lost works

In the collection that has been studied, the most recent 'boutis' is dated 1869. Even if other works were to have been completed here or there, it appears that during the last quarter of the century the handing over of savoir-faire ceased. Mira and Albertine were born around 1850, so we can calculate the time that separates us from the last 'boutisseuses'. For a little girl celebrating her 10th birthday in the year 2000, that represents seven generations, if we allow twenty years for each one.

Why such a long time of cessation? Why have we abandoned a decorative art of such importance, which not only enriches clothing, but also accompanies - with happiness - the sacred moments of life? If there are reasons, they should be good ones, as the disappearance of such a popular art requires explanations. As for evidence, that's another matter. When calico was prohibited, we know that in the past the ban was broken, and that painted fabrics were worn despite the possibility of heavy sanctions: fines, prison or the galleys. In the Languedoc, the Protestant women had to fight to defend their religion; they had to endure corporal punishments, prison and the galleys. So what is this force - as strong as the mistral, on both sides of the Rhone - that caused the disappearance of the 'boutis'?

Several factors seem to be joined together, announcing a deep change in society. It is curious to note that in the following century, all the apprenticeship work, such as needlework, (seams, overcast stitch, flat seams...), embroidery (stitches, samplers, monograms...), or repairs (darns, patching...), have been retransmitted by the mothers, that this female knowledge, just as it did in the sewing room, also has its place in primary school. The boutis did not figure in this, otherwise it would have survived... The war in 1870 seems to be the deadline. During the course of the second half of the century, France endured important economic changes. The railway[19] was installed, improving communications. Industry transformed the structure of society. It was the end of the previously all-powerful manufacturing industries. Another form of working organisation was put in place. The sewing machine appeared, and mechanical stitching offered other interesting padded 'courtepointes'. In this mosaic of changes, fashion changed: the corset and crinoline disappeared. The regional costumes dried up. The designs for the 'boutis' had deteriorated, were used, dispersed, lost, eaten by little mice... The ritual of birth and marriage changed, leaving a place for a new ritual. The white wedding dress still remained; Coco Chanel taught women the fluidity of lines within clothing. The body was liberated, as was the mind...

Women were undertaking other battles too: they were learning how to read and write. The precious time they had spent in creating their 'boutis' was instead spent in cultivating their minds. Learning became the priority.

The 'boutisseuses' were now composing other pages of writing and expressing their feelings and their hopes with other means...

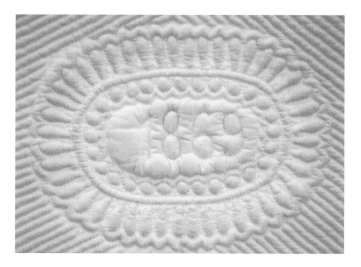

1869: last date visible on the 'boutis' with the sun of flowers. This date signifies the end of an era.

Art and magnificence of the 'boutis'.

134

Other times, other places

During the course of the Middle Ages, the Sicilian 'piquer' workshops had a considerable influence. The crusades transferred techniques to other places that used them in turn, albeit sometimes in a slightly different form. Sardinia and the south of Italy did Trapunto work. The countries of the Orient and of central Europe had been using these techniques for a long time, and still use them today to enrich their precious fabrics. In the 17th and 18th centuries the "piqûres de Marseille", the 'broderie emboutie' which Marseilles made its speciality, were exported throughout Europe, the Indian Ocean, and the Americas. The technique was copied, and gave rise to other 'jupons', other 'courtepointes', whose terminology may be different from our own.

At the time of the Revocation of the Edict of Nantes, many Protestants were exiled, taking their knowledge with them into the Nordic countries[20]. Certain clothes belonging to foreign princes or lords were delicately decorated with 'boutis' embroidery. In the back of beyond in Quebec, the women of Témiscamingue and those of the women of the farmers' circle used 'piquer' frames, similar to ours, and padded their 'couvertures' as in the old days. After the discovery of Canada in 1534 by Jacques Cartier, the emigrants took with them their tools. After five centuries, the pieces are still the same. On the Spanish 'meseta'[21] around Madrid, in the arid areas, the women stuff yellowed cotton into rustic fabrics with the help of small metal tools. In Pouilles, in southern Italy, they use feathers to drive in the stuffing… But the 'boutis' is unique. It is an art. Nowhere other than in Provence or the Languedoc has the perfection that we know been achieved or recognised as part of a regional heritage with such force or presence, and the intelligence and knowledge of the artists of the lower Occitan region passed on.

Pillowcase on which the stitching was completed in 'point de piqûre'.

From Mira to Francine

Decorative art, popular art, the boutis is like a phoenix rising from the ashes. At the dawn of the third millennium, it is a good omen, the sign that we are still holding on to traditional values, that our hands are still capable of creating, that the search for and the idea of beauty are still in our dreams. One and a half centuries separate Mira and Francine, yet they are so close to one another. Love at first sight, a sign of destiny put Francine on the path of the 'boutis', surely because one day, dazzled by so much beauty, her sensitivity sent her out to meet other women, the 'faiseuses de boutis' – this is what the women of Nîmes call the 'boutisseuses' of the Marseilles region.

From Codognan to Calvisson, on the paths of the Garrigue, Francine's footsteps disappear into those of Mira; she smells the same odours, gathers the same flowers; her harvest bouquets combine identical colours. In the little wood of Pasqualet, the odour of the pine trees lives on just as strong, and on the hill with the three mills, the golden broom still sparkles in the sun.

From the spoken and manual handing down of knowledge, the 'boutis' deserves to have its traces recorded; a conservatoire should be created for the works in order to ensure continued handing on to the next generation, and a permanent exhibition should be in the window, to show off the knowledge of our grandparents. Will it also be necessary to have an artistic revival so that other hands can create with the same passion the art of the future, or will this be enough?

It is to answer all these questions that the association 'Les Cordelles, Boutis en Vaunage' was created, so that the women of today, and the little girls of tomorrow can continue the chain with a slight interruption and pass it on in their own time having mastered the technique.

This very specific heritage from the lower Occitan region deserves its proper place, where the documentation and safe-keeping of traditional drawings, and the practising of the art can be next to the miracles of our grandmothers, paying them the respect they are due.

"La Maison du Boutis", Calvisson.

A harvest of 'boutis' on a straw seat.

Poem

Sur la route de Codognan, Mira bourre son boutis.
Au centre de la vane, son soleil fleuri lance, en tournoyant,
Des rayons fous.
Son passe-lacet d'argent glisse une mèche fine
Et la tige se gorge de sève ;
un peu de bourre de coton, la blanche marguerite
s'étale en éventail ;
une bosse de ouate et le cœur de la rose embaume.
Son doigt effleure tendrement le relief du dahlia,
en vérifie le velouté ;
une poussée de boutis… une perle nacrée
va naître de la toile.
À mi-chemin du voyage, les feuilles sortiront « en bosse » ;
à l'arrivée de Beauvoisin, le cœur de sucre battra la chamade.
À l'ombre du micocoulier, sur le vanon de Julie,
Je pique mes fleurs d'amour.
Un peu de fil et je cerne le coquelicot des blés ;
un point arrière, je pointe les pétales du bleuet.
Un petit nœud dans le nid de l'étoffe,
j'emprisonne ses sourires.
Au jardin des Hespérides,
Je cisèle le bouton de rose, et j'adoucis les épines du rameau.
Voici la feuille de chêne pour que sa vie soit éternelle,
L'étoile du firmament, pour que brille l'espérance…
Dans le panier de feuillages et de fruits,
Je lui offre l'abondance

Quelques perles de nacre
Et la grappe jaillit, grain après grain…
Plume après plume,
S'élève le chant du rossignol,
Feuille par feuille, l'ombre se dessine…
Fleur après fleur, je la séduis…
La certitude de mon amour s'écrit en « bosses » de lumière…

Francine Nicolle

NOTES

1. From 'Livre en Broderie' – Bibliothèque Nationale.
2. Ibid.
3. This was everything to do with bed linen and the trousseau.
4. The word 'bed' applies, in this period, to the expensive fabrics that covered it.
5. See 'Les Arts Décoratifs en Provence', Edisud.
6. Saint Aubin in 'L'art du brodeur'.
7. Ibid.
8. Small element made in a series of geometric forms.
9. Cord wound with threads of gold, silver and silk.
10. Strips of cardboard covered with silk or metal thread.
11. Cicada's chirr; the strident cry of the insect.
12. Remove from the vines the branches that are too lush as the leaves are useless.
13. Ibid.
14. Embroidery lamp. A sort of globe of glass on feet placed before a candle, permitting detailed work. See the catalogue from the Arles Exhibition 1998.
15. Little bunches of tightly packed grapes considered to be second grade.
16. Oil lamps hung on the mantelpiece, for example.
17. A small piece of furniture to put the glasses in/on.
18. The sisters of this convent made bridal 'jupons' during their time of penitence.
19. Sections of railways were put down and soldered in place between Paris and Marseilles in 1858.
20. Under the wigs that the nobility wore, hair was cut, close cropped. Inside they wore bonnets to keep out the cold. Some nightcaps, in linen, were made in Northern Germany in the 18th century.
21. Mountainous plateau.

Conclusion

Threads that have come from abroad have woven a history, and fabrics that have served as a support to the stitching techniques have found their value on the shores of the Mediterranean. The land of the Lower Occitan region has given a cultural and linguistic framework to the exceptional art of the 'boutis'. Fashioned like a jewel and polished over time by the hands of women, the 'boutis' captured its gloriousness the moment it became a regional treasure. Present in the works that have punctuated the important moments of life, it has become, over time, a popular art: as a costume, it delivered a certificate of recognition/acknowledgement; the tradition will last for eternity.

Gestures repeated a thousand times, from the intelligence of men, have permitted the creation of textiles destined to envelop the body with warmth, cleanliness and beauty. Linen and hemp, silk and cotton were to further embellish the 'boutis', seducing us in the process. Thanks to the blooming floral ornamentation, a picture language 'en-bosses' was the first writing in stitches marked on fabric, offering us wonderful stories of love, wisdom and gallantry, recounting the life of men.

The first fabric manuscripts embroidered in 'boutis', in relief, were to rub shoulders with other parchment manuscripts with precious illuminations.

The floral embellishments and the symbols used have created a personal language that is quite secret and difficult to decipher. Skilful, precise hands have modelled a relief and played with the contrasts of light and shadow to fashion these dreamy 'boutis'. The motifs created by the hand of man depict curves, raised areas and forms taken either from imagination or drawn from the environment, which shows creative sensitivity as the hand has not yet learnt to obey a machine - man is still his own master. His intelligence, sensitive to his needs, proposes different stitching techniques, dictated by climatic or economic reasons, depending on whether he lives in the town or the country, near to the Mediterranean coast or the mountain foothills. The opportunity, or lack of opportunity, for obtaining the raw materials (textiles, cotton wadding, thread,) as well as the availability of tools modified a technique that was already adaptable, depending on the natural resources. This multitude of variants gave rise to a mosaic of 'boutis', all of which are different, but all obeying the identical rule of fabrication; this mosaic copies exactly another mosaic, that of a multitude of little countries, where, from one garrigue to another, little peculiarities are visible, minor differences, which define the charm of each one.

From the stitching workshops of the Middle Ages, the 'boutis' has seduced, in turn, each level of society and all religions. At the end of the 18th century, it was to be claimed as a right by women, who were to take over the savoir-faire and pass it on, preferably in secret, from one generation to the next. In this slow democratisation of the social classes, the arrival of cotton was to help them in this intuitive process. Besides, how would they have continued the 'boutis' without cotton? The stitching act is to be considered on its own, as stitched works have always existed throughout the centuries, next to wool 'couvertures' and feather eiderdowns, which give stitching a very special place. The 'boutis', from its spoken and manual tradition of transmitting the savoir-faire, was to disappear little by little with the arrival of writing and the decline of the Oc language. In the second half of the 19th century, the industrial movement is not enough to explain why our grandmothers, faithful to our tradition, consented to abandon this popular art, whose beauty touches us and fills our souls with wonder. In this movement, at the end of the century, our elders had to make other choices; in giving education the priority, they finally learnt how to read and write, creating a boundary to the period closing the chapter in another way…

To take up the torch again is to pay a justified and merited homage to all those 'faiseuses de boutis', as, most of the time, it was the 'boutisseuses' in the country who made the 'boutis' for the towns. Our generations, who in turn master the knowledge, need to locate their old values, as well as their creative side. In a world that has levelled out, returning to our origins has proved to be beneficial.

What sense shall we give to our fabric parchments? What horizons will our thread embroider? In a blink of an eye, we have moved into a worldwide place… We have so many tales to embroider 'en bosses'!

And what if we recapture, in the style of the troubadours, the stories of cotton, embroidered in 'boutis' in which man knows only of love?

"Madame de Maintenon embroidered all over the place, and in every place, during coach journeys and during council with the King."

On her cart taking her to Beauvoisin, Mira was stitching her 'couverton' in 'boutis'…

In the TGV (high speed train) or on a plane, I 'boutisse' Julie's 'vanon'…

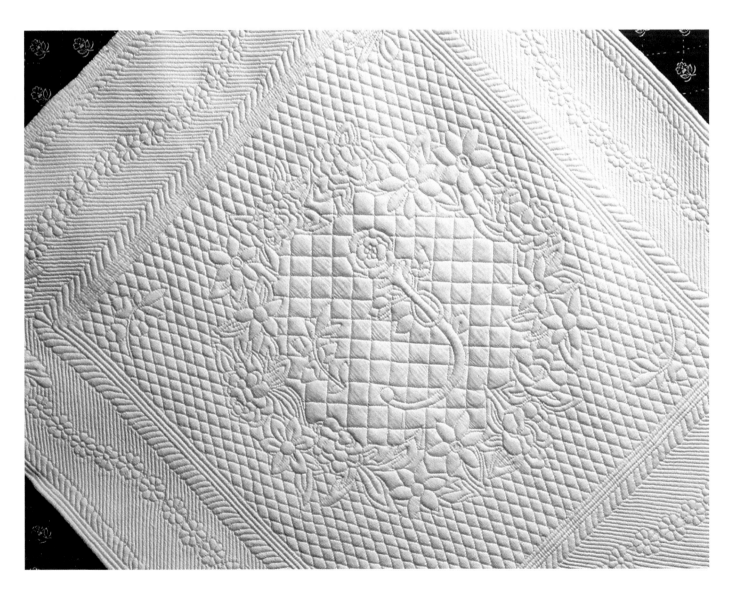

Practical section

Initiation to the 'boutis'

1. Choice of fabrics

"D'autro pougnent la telo fino" "Others stitch fine fabrics"
Frédéric Mistral

In the past, cotton or silk of different thickness was used, depending on what the piece was to be used for.

"The 'Boutis', Work Divine" F. Mistral.

Here are the textiles quoted most frequently in exhibition catalogues or from the collections studied.

For the topside:

Precious works:

- Silk
- Lawn
- Nansouk
- Chiffon

More ordinary, or more solid works:

- Basin
- Percale
- Stiff percale
- Printed calico
- Cotton fabric
- Calico

For the underside

- Household linen
- Cotton and linen mix
- Futaine
- Basin
- Stiff percale
- Rouan (cotton)

Colours

- 90% white (mainly cotton)
- 10% colour

dominant colours:

royal blue, sunflower yellow
(coloured 'boutis' were made in silk).

In comparison with stitched 'couvertures' – padded – the real 'boutis' of white fabric can be recognised from their transparency. Placed against the light, the light can travel along the lines of stitching, which is not the case with anything padded, as the surface remains opaque.

This process of identification can prove useful if a purchase is to be made in a market…

In the present day, many of the fabrics are no longer made. To make a pretty boutis, the fabric must be new; ordinary cotton should be avoided as the 'boutis' is an art; its' embellishments need a great deal of time spent on them; it is often given as a present and should survive several generations. It would be better to choose a beautiful and pure cotton:

- a beautiful percale
- an Egyptian cotton
- lawn

1. The fabric is not washed.

2. Avoid cotton fabrics that are too thick as they are difficult to stitch.

3. If you choose two different fabrics (for example a fine lawn for the top and a normal cotton fabric for the bottom), put them back to back and selvage to selvage, to give them the same direction.

4. The work will lose 10 to 15% of its size after it has been stuffed and washed, so you should work out your sizes beforehand.

5. Allow 10cm on each side so that the embroidery hoop can be placed satisfactorily, or sew lengths of material to each side, enlarging the piece for the moment.

2. Preparation

Necessary materials

– Fabric

– A table and an iron

– A large ruler

– An HB pencil

A good piece of work requires patience, method, good tools and good materials.

In the past, did they iron the fabric? Without a doubt.

In the present day, it must be done (don't use steam) in order to have a flat surface and to be able to prepare the marks.

Advice for beginners:

– It is better to use the **same** fabric for both sides (50cm x 100cm).

– Cut the warp **perpendicular to the selvege.**

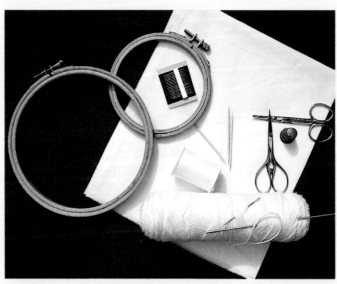

Cotton fabric and the tufts of cotton, short sewing needles are the tools for succeeding.

Simple actions

– Fold in two (back to back) and then iron. You should have a square of 50cm x 50cm.

– Fold vertically in half and iron the fold.

– Fold horizontally in half. This is how you locate the centre of your work. Mark it with a wooden pencil.

– Open up the fabric and mark the folds with a pencil. Be careful that the crayon is not too hard (HB no2, or similar). These are your lines to locate everything by.

They are not stitched and they will disappear in the wash.

They serve for positioning the motifs, tracing the framework or the vermicelli (parallel channels which are stitched and stuffed).

Location lines.

Choosing the motifs

– Fall in love with a motif… and visualise the result!

– The design is drawn on the right side of the fabric.

– The chosen motif can be placed in the centre… or not (see further on the compositions for the 'pétasson' or the 'vane').

– Be inspired by the list of proposed motifs and patterns to complete the works in "the spirit of the Provencal 'boutis'". Then, place your symbols on the fabric – if there is enough room.

The symbol should not take over the whole piece and spoil the aesthetics. Too many symbols ruin the meaning. Don't put anything on without knowing its meaning (see the chapter on motifs and symbols and its dictionary). As to the initials, you shouldn't go wrong!

The transferring of the motif.

In the past, we had stencils, models on paper for silk or stiff percale, which was perforated with the help of a bodkin or a tracing wheel. The stencil was placed on the right side of the fabric, and then the surface was rubbed with a tracing powder so that the powder would pass through the holes onto the fabric. After the stencil was removed, the outlines were traced with a pencil, and a fine spray of alcohol was passed over the top, fixing the design (see photo).

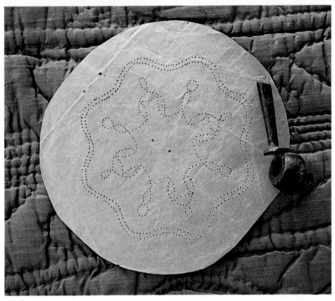

Perforated stencil accompanied by its alcohol pipette.
To obtain identical stencils, several sheets of paper were placed on top
of each other and perforated together.

In the present day, there are various and more modern ways of completing the above.

– The easiest way is to transfer the motif using tracing paper: Stick the motif to the table, an artist's board or on a large piece of flat cardboard. A lit table can also be used, especially for coloured cottons.

– Open out the fabric and place on top of the paper motif, taking care to place the central lines on top of those on the paper (follow those from the iron and those that have been drawn on).

– Stick the sides of the fabric down using moveable sticky tape.

– Start to draw the central motif from top to bottom, to avoid dirtying the fabric (don't use a thick pencil – HB n°2 or 0.5 lead is advised).

– When the motif is drawn, spray the surface with alcohol (sold in a spray in pharmacies).

Tracing the drawing should be fine, neat and precise.

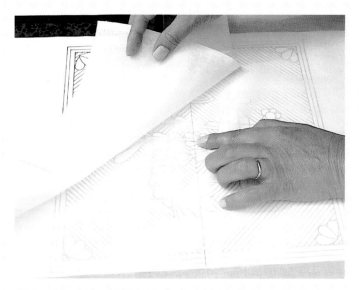

Place, with precision, the location lines on the drawing and with those on the fabric.

The background

– Trace parallel lines directly onto the fabric (using the pre-pared model); or draw a pattern that you can slide underneath the fabric when you have removed the motif.

Remember do not draw over the motif with the vermicelli (if you make a mistake, leave it as will wash out).

– Draw on your lines with a transparent ruler in such a way that the drawn lines are visible as you move the ruler.

– There are all sorts of vermicelli: 2, 3, 4, 5… 8mm in width! On the diagonal, on the warp, both directions alternately, in a "mistralade"…

– There are surfaces associated with the vermicelli:
  • Little squares (sides of 1cm or less),
  • Little lozenges (1cm or less),
  • Larger squares (sides not more than 2cm),
  • In arcs (drawn towards the interior, the centre or the exterior).

– Sometimes the motifs follow into each other and do not particularly require a background. In this case, it is **a real 'piqué de Marseille'**. The word still exists in modern French, and incorrectly describes stitched 'couvertures'… where there is confusion…

– *If you make a mistake*, do not rub it out with an eraser, even a textile eraser. It is possible to correct little errors with a fine blue dressmakers pen, sold in specialised shops (to be washed after – **without question** – in cold water).

3. The tacking

– At this stage, when the design has been completely trans-ferred (motif, framework and vermicelli), the two pieces of fabric must be tacked together in large running stitch.

– The thread must be the same colour as the fabric (use the same as the one you will use for the stitches later).

– Start tacking at the sides, not in the middle.

– Either having made a knot, or done a backstitch, stitch in a cross a little way from the central lines, and around the framework.

– If it is a large piece, then repeat this every 10 to 15cm, which will help prevent the piece from becoming deformed.

– A tacking stitch should not pull. If this is the case, cut a stitch to give it some slack.

4. The embroidery hoop

In the past, an embroidery hoop was used (also called an embroidery frame) for all embroidery stitches and probably for the 'boutis' on the workshops.

It is in looking at finished works that the difference can be seen. The result is more beautiful when the fabric was stretched for the stitching and for the stuffing.

There were large frames, mounted on feet, others that were placed on trestle tables, but they cannot have been that practical.

In the present day, using an embroidery hoop or frame is advised. Five minutes a day is enough to get the hang of it. Be courageous… it is the same for the thimble (which is worn on the middle finger!).

A little hoop of 8 to 10cm in diameter is light and man-ageable, suitable for little motifs – flowers and leaves.

When you are an expert, you will be able to use larger hoops with ease…

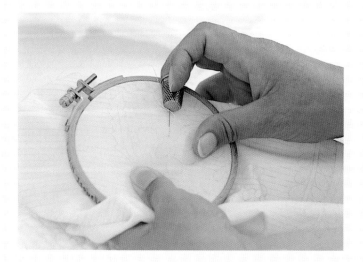

STITCHES USED

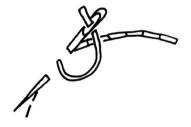

POINT DE PIQÛRE – BACKSTITCH

Pull the needle through on the line of the design, go back a stitch, and bring the needle through in front of and to the left of the first stitch. To complete another stitch, put the needle through the hole that it made the first time.

POINT DEVANT AND POINT DEVANT DOUBLE – RUNNING STITCH, AND DOUBLE RUNNING STITCH.

Double running stitch is created after the first 'run' has been completed. A second thread, the same as the first, completes a second 'run' inside the first.

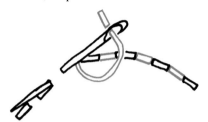

POINT DE NOEUD – FRENCH KNOT

Pull the thread through at the desired point, holding the thread under the left thumb, and circle the needle once or twice with the thread. Holding the circled thread tightly, bring them down towards the base of the needle, near the beginning of the thread, and pull gently. Take the needle through near the stitch, and bring it up wherever you want.

The size of the knot will depend on how many times you circle the needle with the thread.

POINT DE FESTON – BLANKET STITCH

Bring the needle through on the lower line and start to take the needle through the upper line, bringing it back through on the lower line in a vertical movement, having placed the thread under the needle. Pull the stitch in order to form a loop, and start again. The stitches should be tightly packed one against another. This stitch being used in embroidery should have the loops on the outside edge of the piece. Use short, sharp scissors with pointed blades, and cut with care. This stitch can be used in various cases.

POINT DE CHAÎNETTE – CHAIN STITCH

Pull the thread through on the line being followed and hold the thread under the left thumb. Put the needle back in, near where it first came out, just underneath it. Pull the thread under the needle and pull the needle through. Continue.

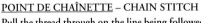

Right

wrongride

POINT DE BÂTI – TACKING STITCH

There are two techniques.

The first is done on the right side and the second is done on the wrong side meaning that only little stitches appear on the right side.

5. The stitching

To stitch is to sew the two layers of fabric together.
Stitching was and still is, done by hand.

In the past, our grandmothers used several different sorts of stitches.

Here is a list of stitches found from the collection studied:
– Point de piqûre – the oldest form used until the 19th century
– Point arrière – similar to backstitch, only a gap appears between each stitch
– Point de chaînette – see sketch
– Point avant – same as 'point devant'
– Point avant double – same as 'point devant double'
– Mixture of 'point de piqûre' and 'point avant'

In the present day, the 'point avant' was the most rapid stitch, but the 'point de pîqure' could be used for the centre of a heart, a small detail…

The 'geste'

– The stitching starts at the centre of the piece. Each designed motif should be stitched on the line of the design.
  Remember: the construction lines are not to be stitched.
– The stitch should be small and should be done in such a way as to really compartmentalize each motif; in this way, the cotton stuffing cannot escape.
– The stitch should be smaller than that of the stuffing.
– Take a threaded needle – no more than 40cm – as well as a stitching needle.
– Make a flat knot (one loop); leave 2cm of thread after the knot.
– Insert the needle away from the start point.
– Thread the needle between the two layers of fabric; bring it out on a line of the motif.
– Pull the thread hard to close off the knot: keep it away from the stitching line – it will prevent it from coming out: leave it 2mm from the inside. If the knot is stuck, pull

it back with the little 'tail' of thread. If there is a problem, do not make a knot.
– Do a small backstitch, and start the stitching.
The stitching improves with practice… that's the secret!
The quality of the wadding depends on the quality of the stitching.

The stitching is done on the large motifs, starting from the centre.

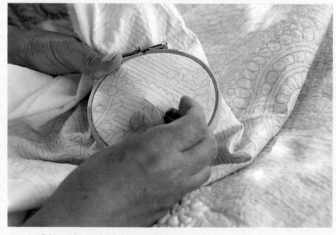

Be careful to take up both layers of fabric.

A little advice

– *Mark in a book the sizes of your frames before stitching.*
– *Make sure you stitch both layers of fabric, and check the back from time to time (especially at the beginning). The stitching should be regular. Don't rush… it will come.*
– *To avoid hurting your finger underneath, place it carefully on the vertical… the needle will but up against the nail (or… protect it).*
– *When stitching a motif is finished, you can start stitching the next motif, as long as it does not cross the threads (which will become an obstacle when it comes to the wadding); you need to slide the needle the length of the stitching between the two layers of fabric.*
– *Stitch the motifs starting from the centre, then, little by little, towards the edge.*

PATTERN – STITCHING – INITIATION

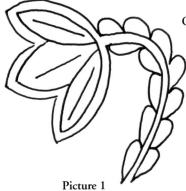

Order of stitching for this type of shape:

- The centre of the stem
- The links to the contour of the Iris
- Sew the interior of the Iris
- Sew the veins
- Sew the little leaves on the stem.

Picture 1

Order of stitching

1. Large motifs, starting from the centre
2. The frames or the festooned borders
3. The 'vermicelli'

This order is preferable; it avoids a deformation of the frame.

In case the frame is enlarged, the fault must be rectified in the sewing; it is necessary to complete each side separately. Having stitched one side, gather gently together in order to return to the original measurements...or thereabouts. Repeat for each side.

Picture 2

Trick to prevent the thread being cut too often

← Direction of the sewing

← When the stitching of the first petal is finished

SLIDE AGAINST THE STITCHING BETWEEN THE TWO LAYERS OF FABRIC AND EXIT AT A.

Stitch each of the petals in this way.

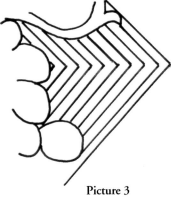

Picture 3

Stitching the vermicelli.

Slide the needle between the two layers of fabric, against the stitching and outside the grain or petal (in order to keep the form of the curve).

When the occasion arises, stitch the grains at the same time as the vermicelli.

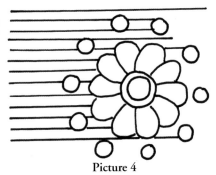

Picture 4

Picture 5

Order of sewing: -

1. Sew the central circle. Stop stitching.
2. Sew the second circle.
3. Continue with the petals as shown in picture 2.

REMEMBER: do not cross from one shape to the next with the thread whilst sewing, in order not to leave an obstacle when filling with cotton during the wadding stage.

6. The stuffing or wadding

The relief of the motifs is obtained by introducing spun cotton (as used for knitting) between the two layers of fabric.

The expression "broderie de l'intérieur" therefore, is totally justified.

In the past, on embroidered works in 'boutis', the relief was obtained with the help of tufts of spun cotton (often found) or of cotton wadding (more rare).

The tufts were either pushed or pulled.

If we look carefully at the 'boutis' needle, two eyes are noticeable, the smaller for threading the spun cotton, and the larger for thicker tufts.

The bodkin had the same role.

The edge swollen with the needle was used to push the tuft once it has been cut. When the tuft was too short, it was necessary to add a little more.

Stuffing and wadding were done from the reverse side. **It is certain** that the work was or was not stretched on a hoop.

The most beautiful 'boutis' have an **impeccable** reverse as the tufts were carefully entered; they were also stretched on a frame (embroidery hoop).

A 'boutis' is practically reversible; there should be no holes visible on the reverse.

What were the bodkins for?

They were…

– for making a hole before pushing the cotton tufts into the motif

– to push the cotton in equally (into a corner…)

– to make the tuft follow a 'vermicelli' – in this case, the fabric is stitched then the tuft is pushed in little by little, and then on the inside of the 'vermicelli' a snaking tuft is obtained rather than a straight line.

Assortment of bodkins of all types.

In the present day, the relief on the motifs is obtained by introducing cotton (type used for knitting) between the two layers of fabric.

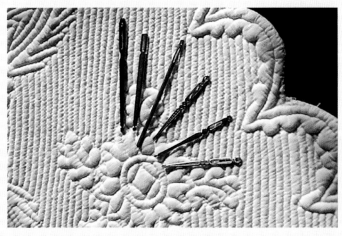

'Boutis' needles of various sizes, precious or modest.
The rounded end served to push in the tuft.

Different stages in the fabrication of cotton.
The top left is cotton wadding, followed by the refining of the tufts.

149

The materials

– The cotton should be 100% cotton. Cotton mixed with synthetics becomes grey along the length, yellows, and cannot support bleaching.

– The tufts should be a little twisted in such a way that it opens and relaxes inside, just like the original flower. Two strands should be used; therefore high diameter cotton should be avoided which would make irreparable holes in the fabric, especially if it is fine.

Advice: choose cotton that is used for knitting that would be used with number 4 needles or thereabouts.

The tools

– A tapestry needle number 18 or 16, and no other. This replaces the 'boutis' needle.

– A 'trapunto' needle (optional: sold in shops which specialise in patchwork).

– An embroidery hoop.

– Small nail scissors, curved towards the top, or embroidery scissors.

– Wooden cocktail sticks.

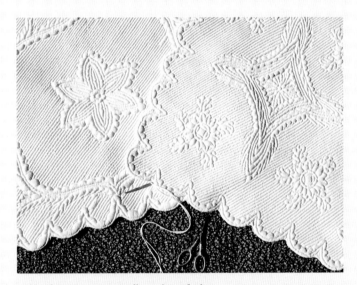

A number 18 tapestry needle works perfectly.

Unfinished works in 'boutis' teach us many things

– When the coats of arms were placed in the centre, the medallion was left empty. It was filled after the order was placed (see *Les Arts décoratifs en Provence,* Edisud) so it was left until last (both in stitching and in padding), but was still professionally completed…

– For the rest, the stitching on the piece should have been completely finished before undertaking its wadding: that's for certain.

– The 'faiseuses de boutis' started by filling the large motifs; they did not start at the centre! It was the base of the piece (or a corner), which served as a departure point. Then. The wadding progressed using common sense towards the top or the sides.

Using the hoop

– It is advised to wad* and to stuff* using a hoop. (Mira used a little frame).

– The stitching finished, turn the piece over. To make the work easier, start in the centre. Place the loop (the metallic side on the wrong side this time).

– The size of the hoops used varies… The smallest (around 10cm in diameter) is ideal when a flower or small motif is being padded.

– Use larger and larger hoops or plastic square frames (30 – 50cm in width).

*wad = stuff (the latter suggests larger motifs, but it is the same action).

Attention: at any given moment, you will have to place your frame on motifs that are already filled. Position it, even force it, then tighten the screw securely. The cotton will be battered and flattened in an instant, but it will take its initial volume later. Washing will arrange the rest…

Remember: when you stretch the fabric, don't pull it on the bias or at the corners.

For the wadding, the hoop is placed on the wrong side of the work.

Advice

– Start by filling the motifs at the centre of the piece (motifs or vermicelli).
– Proceed, as with the stitching, by heading towards the edges in all directions (sometimes it is easier to wad the vermicelli between the motifs as you go, especially if they are small).

The large motifs are finished.

The wadding of the large motifs in the centre.

The progression in the large motifs.

Wadding of the vermicelli, starting from the centre.

151

WADDING – INITIATION

Simple forms – The first passage

Round

Oval

Choose the longest side.
Start on the central axis.

Ring (anneau)

Pass the thread through several times (5).
The thread is cut each time. Start from
behind the previous exit point.

Pointed and Leaves Petals

Pass the cotton thread from the base of
the leaf or the petal towards the point.

The cotton thread should
place itself either side of the
central vein.

Round Petals

Fill from the base towards
the top of the petal. Start
from the centre.
Follow the direction of the
arrows to avoid passing
through the same hole.

Geometric forms

Choose the longest axis

To wad the basket: Start from the central square and
work towards the outside.

Borders and Curves

Exit each time you feel the need arises and cut the thread.

Cut the thread.
Start again from behind
the last exit point, as
for the ring
shown above.

**To achieve a well rounded motif, a second layer of stuffing needs to be
applied to the same area, in the same direction as the first, by lifting up
the fabric.**

The actions

– For the motifs, double the cotton tuft. For that pass the tuft through the eye of the needle, pull until you have equal lengths – you now have a double strand.

– Squash, with your fingers, the fold on the cotton in order to help the first passage. The tapestry needle should work well as the point is neither too rounded nor too sharp.

– The cotton tuft will sit inside the motif (the line of stitching will determine the edge). Start, and stay close, to the stitching **on the inside** of the motif, and exit close to the stitching **inside** the motif.

On a small hoop or frame

– With the end of the needle, lift up one layer of fabric, slide the needle into the motif and pull the thread as indicated, until it almost disappears. (See photo and sketch).

– Cut carefully 1 or 2mm from the motif.

– With the cocktail stick, delicately push the tuft into the motif from both ends.

– Repeat the same action on the motif close to the first passage. Avoid using the same hole.

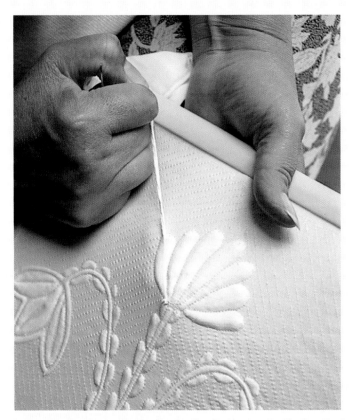

Pull on the tuft until it almost disappears.

Passing the needle through the length of the petal.

Cut with care, the scissors parallel to the fabric.

The wadding is easier stretched on a frame.

To pass through the second layer, guide the end of the needle toward the top; it should puff up the fabric from the inside. At this point, hold firmly, between the thumb and the index finger, the motif you are in the process of wadding, whilst passing through the second tuft, (in order to avoid a muddle.)

– *It is permitted to tamp down the cotton with the needle in order to have an interesting first layer of stuffing.*
– *To obtain a relief, more 'en bosse', it is necessary to pass – in the same direction – a second layer of wadding over the top of the first, by lifting the fabric, as best possible, with the help of the needle.*

Evaluation of the wadding

It should be pleasing to both the touch and the eye.
– *To the touch*: the motifs should be solid between the two fingers. Put light pressure on – it should not be "soft".
– *To the eye*: do not forget… it is a sculpture, like the 'bas-relief'.

On the other hand, washing will compact the interior cotton and tamp it down further. Anticipate this shrinkage…

The extremities of the tufts are pushed in with care, little by little, and not at the end.

Perfecting

"Practice leads to perfection."

1. The stitching

- Be vigilant when stitching the two layers.
- Use enough thread to complete your vermicelli.
- Start your vermicelli or motif with a backstitch.
- Use a number 12 needle if your eyesight is good enough.
- Avoid slackening the fabric along the length of your vermicelli: if it is too loose, gather it gently to compensate for the fold.
- In points and corners, make two consecutive 'points de piqûre' in order to edge the shape, (see the drawing.)

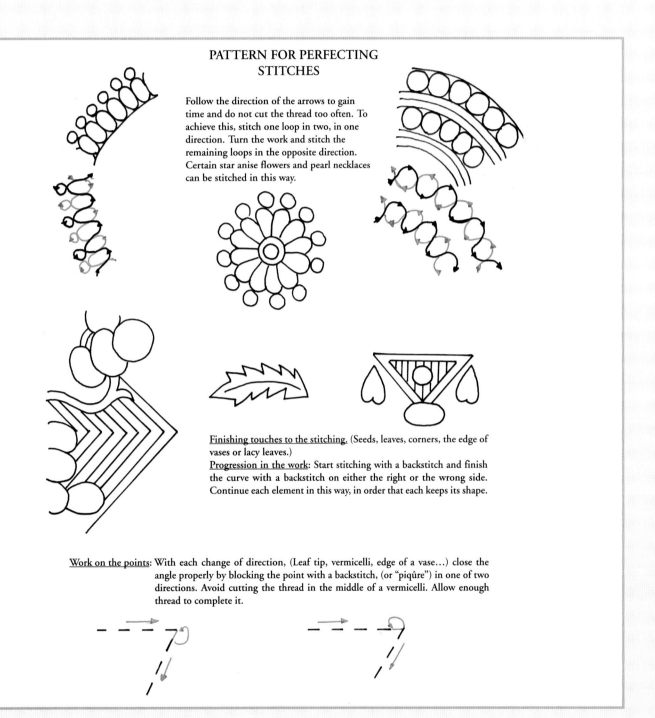

PATTERN FOR PERFECTING STITCHES

Follow the direction of the arrows to gain time and do not cut the thread too often. To achieve this, stitch one loop in two, in one direction. Turn the work and stitch the remaining loops in the opposite direction. Certain star anise flowers and pearl necklaces can be stitched in this way.

<u>Finishing touches to the stitching.</u> (Seeds, leaves, corners, the edge of vases or lacy leaves.)

<u>Progression in the work</u>: Start stitching with a backstitch and finish the curve with a backstitch on either the right or the wrong side. Continue each element in this way, in order that each keeps its shape.

<u>Work on the points</u>: With each change of direction, (Leaf tip, vermicelli, edge of a vase...) close the angle properly by blocking the point with a backstitch, (or "piqûre") in one of two directions. Avoid cutting the thread in the middle of a vermicelli. Allow enough thread to complete it.

2. The wadding and the padding

- STUFFING – REACHING PERFECTION –
SIMPLE FORMS – SECOND COTTON FILLING

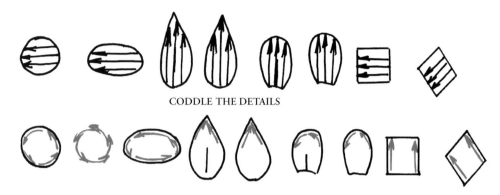

CODDLE THE DETAILS

GENTLE CURVES

Obligatory exit of the tuft.
Cut.

Possibilities of using the "lasso"

Passage of the tuft once.

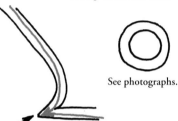

See photographs.

Exit of the tufts.

Pass the tuft from the base of the vermicelli towards the point – exit – cut –
Push it in with a cocktail stick.
Continue in the same way in the other direction.
Always exit at the point.
Cut – push in the tuft.
Finish all the vermicelli.
If you feel that the points need more cotton, delicately place another tuft, following the direction of the arrow. (See the drawing.)

TO SCULPT A FLOWER

Wadding with a needle permits the flowers to be sculpted. Inside the motif, it is possible to give more volume to the centre of the flower or to the petals.
In this way, from one flower to the next, the petals and the centres can be modified.

For a grape, it is possible to overfill the centre in comparison to the edge.

ORDER OF STUFFING

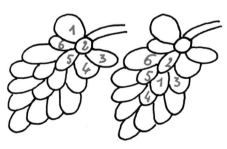

Start at the base of the motif and then work your way up. Or start at the centre and work outwards in all directions.

DIRECTION OF WADDING

<u>Grapes, pearl necklaces:</u>

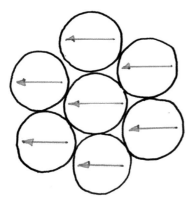
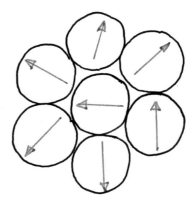

The direction can be identical   or   it can change direction from one grape to the next.

<u>Flowers:</u>

The centre of the flower can be wadded in one direction, (of your choice,) but the petals are always wadded from the base to the tip.

- Pass your two layers of filling in the same direction.
- Complete each motif, as is indicated in the picture inserts. Your needle is the artist's paintbrush; it can add cotton anywhere where there is not enough, (must be done right next to the stitching, and not destroy the order of the interior wadding.) Hold the piece up to the light and note the areas where wadding is missing.
- It is possible to only pass one strand of cotton into delicate areas, or to separate the strand.
- In case of "boudifle"* visible on the reverse, stitch this granule with a cocktail stick and move the cotton through with a circular movement.
- **Do not forget that the hand is also a tool... and so are fingers and nails (if you have them).**
- "Feel," from underneath, the work with your left hand.
- Stop the tapestry needle from going through to the other side.
- Hold the motif with the thumb and index finger whilst wadding... when this is possible.
- Press out a "boudifle" or a hole, by rubbing it with a nail.
  * "Boudifle" is a regional word, used to explain the swelling produced by a mosquito bite.

The cocktail stick, on the right side, gets rid of irregular wadding swellings

The reverse

The reverse of old 'boutis' tell us what tools were used. It also enlightens us to the methods used.

In the past, the intervals between the holes show the needles used were of different lengths and did not fulfil the same functions; using the bodkin was frequent.
- Only one hole in the motif... the tuft was pushed.
- Two holes... the needle passed from one end to the other; the tuft in this case was pushed from each side.
- No hole visible... the fabric was of good quality; the 'boutis' needlewomen had experience; she knew her art.

- More important holes along the length of the vermicelli show that the tuft was pulled out, that it was put back in through the same hole: the needle was too short, the hole remained open.

Today, the tapestry needle has replaced the bodkin, to our advantage. With the 'lasso' (see later) the holes are minimised.

The trapunto needle is practical for wadding certain vermicelli in one go. Combined with the 'lasso', long distances can easily be worked, (frames, borders).
- **Your tufts should be carefully entered.**
  For that cut at 1 or 2 mm outside the motif and with the cocktail stick, push the end in carefully, (the pushing action should be horizontal, on the bias, or in a spiral...).
- **Close your holes...** by scratching the fibres of the fabric with a cocktail stick or a fingernail... washing will do the rest.

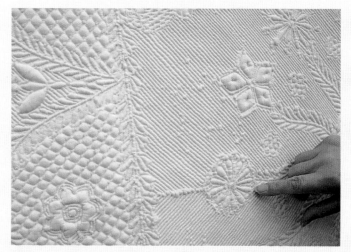

The tuft has crossed the motif from side to side. On the vermicelli, the holes show the gaps and indicate the entrance and exit in the same hole.

Only one hole: the tuft was pushed in.

3. Straight borders

They were used on certain 'vanes', 'pétassons' and bridal 'jupons'.

Made with several vermicelli, they were often bordered with lace or crochet, broderie anglaise or embroidered chiffon.

On the most beautiful 'boutis' these borders do not buckle!

It is during the preparation stage of the piece and during the stitching that faults are to be avoided… not afterwards!

Advice:

– Allow a larger surface of material than that of the work, (20cm all around): In this way, the hoop, placed on the border, will not deform, or sew the provisional borders which will increase the work surface.

– Make your tacking tighter and closer.

– In case of little undulations, correct the fault by 'gathering' the line of stitches together; from time to time, put in a backstitch to block the thread.

4. The simplest part: the hem

The ideal is to trace the cutting line at the same time as sketching the design.

– Trace, with a ruler, a frame of about 8 or 9 mm from the last vermicelli.

– Cut at the same time the two layers of fabric, and on the reverse, sew a normal hem which will give a final, fatter vermicelli.

– Fold 4 or 5 mm, then another 5 mm. Pin…, tack…, and sew in running stitches or sliding stitches along the groove. The stitch should be invisible on the reverse.

– Profit from this last occasion to correct a final fault: Pull gently on the thread of the hem in order to rectify the dimensions.

Another possibility: overcasting.

It is rarer and not as beautiful as hemming, which gives a flat border.

– Fold again towards the interior, each part of the fabric, by 3 or 4 mm. (Avoid stretching the fabric!).

– Pin and sew using tiny invisible stitches.

– WAD this last vermicelli.

Finally, wash your 'boutis'.

Leave half a centimetre of tufted cotton outside each of the corners, then delicately push in, in order to fill the space.

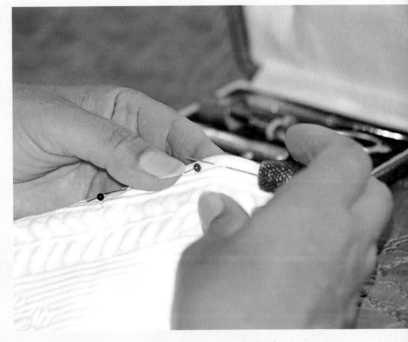

Hemming is a good finish: it gives a smooth aspect to the border.

5. Adding lace or 'broderie anglaise'

Lace and 'broderie anglaise' is placed against the last vermicelli on straight or scalloped borders on a 'pétasson' and on straight borders on a 'vane'.

Lace

– Cut the fabric 6mm around the entire piece.
– Tack the lace. Eventually, fold it lightly, as with the 'broderie anglaise'. (See photo.)
– Gather more generously on the corners, in order to correctly change direction.
– Stitch in the old style with small running or sliding stitches.

On the reverse

– Turn the work.
– Fold back the material that is cut towards the base.
– Re-cut it carefully.
– Place, straddling the fabric, a neat braid of 4 or 5 mm wide, to hide the fold and to have a perfect finish.
– Sew this braid with little running stitches, without crossing the two layers of fabric.

'Broderie anglaise'

In the past, it was put on the right side, having prepared a small fold on the base of the 'broderie anglaise'.

In the present day, it is better to fold gently, then tack the right side against the right side, folding more in the corners, against the last vermicelli.

– Sew with running or backstitch.
– Re-cut, if necessary, the layers of fabric, to 5 mm. Fold them towards the base… pin… tack.
– Place a neat braid and not on the bias, of 4 or 5 mm in width, straddling the cut… sew with small running stitches.

6. The 'lasso'

This is a technique used in the large embroidery schools and also by electricians, cobblers and plumbers, to pass thread into a sheath.

This procedure allows:

– To wad long lengths of vermicelli without having holes on the wrong side. (See photograph of the 'lasso' and its use.)
– Complete all of the gentle curves.
– To use them in rings, on the condition that the work is perfectly stretched on the hoop. Circles, for example, can be wadded in two goes. (A half circle, then the other.)
– This 'coupling' can prolong a tapestry or trapunto needle.

The 'pétasson' from Arles shows a beautiful 'broderie anglaise' of four fingers in width.

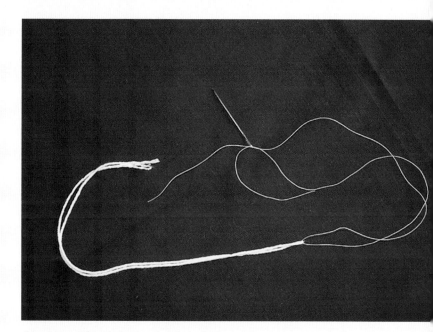

Mounting used in the large embroidery schools.

7. The mounting

– Take a solid quilting thread of approximately 40 to 50 cms in length.
– Fold it in two.
– Thread the two strands through the eye of a needle; make a **knot** at the eye of the needle, then another.
– In this way, a hoop can be achieved, through which the tuft of cotton can be passed. Fold this tuft, then press down on the fold with the finger, to facilitate its entrance into the fabric.

Choice of needle for this mounting.

The points of tapestry and trapunto needles are perfect.
– A pointed needle sticks to the inside of the fabric.
– A rounded needle struggles to pierce the fabric.

8. Scalloped borders of 'pétassons' or 'vanes'.

These scallops can be more or less pronounced.

Everything that has a rounded form or in hoops poses a problem, and in particular, necklines, as therein reside difficulties.

The 'boutis' needle women got round this by placing a braid which served to consolidate the edges, or by using blanket stitch.

Closures on the hem were reserved, most of the time, for wadded works.

Some 'pétassons' that are particularly worked, present a scalloped border, garnished with 'broderie anglaise', which is three fingers in width…

Depending on your choice, the progress of the operation will be different.

A braid is not of the "bias"… it resembles a hook, but it is straighter, (4 to 6 mm in width). **It should be steeped beforehand, as it must remain supple.**

'Pétasson' from Nîmes.

Scalloped borders bring out the elegance of the model.

Blanket stitch

Blanket stitch is embroidered having finished all of the stitching. (See photo and advice for completing this stitch.) On the border of the 'vane', this stitch should be no more than 2 or 3 mm in height.

Placing of the braid

The braid is placed once the work has been finished. (This is to say, after the wadding is completed.)

It is found on the wrong side of the 'pétassons', rarely straddling, or on the right side. (See how to place it after the photo.)

– Cut the two layers of fabric 5 mm from the last vermicelli, avoiding going too far into the neckline. The braid will not perfectly marry the shapes, but in this way, it avoids lumpiness.

The placing is on the right side

– Pin the braid near to the last vermicelli, between 1/2 or 1 mm from the last line of stitching. (See insert.)

– Sew in little running stitches, (of the old style,) or invisible stitches.

– Fold back to the wrong side; pin carefully in the round areas, to absorb any fullness in the fabric. Tack if necessary.

– Sew in little running stitches, or invisible stitches, by gathering your thread; only through one layer of fabric.

In the case of adding flouncing 'broderie anglaise' this should first be placed right side against right side, the braid placed on the wrong side, hiding the final cut of the fabric, on the 'pétassons' and the base of the 'broderie anglaise'.

PLACING OF A BRAID

CUT OF THE FABRIC:

—— Line of cut for both layers of fabric.

PLACING OF THE BRAID:

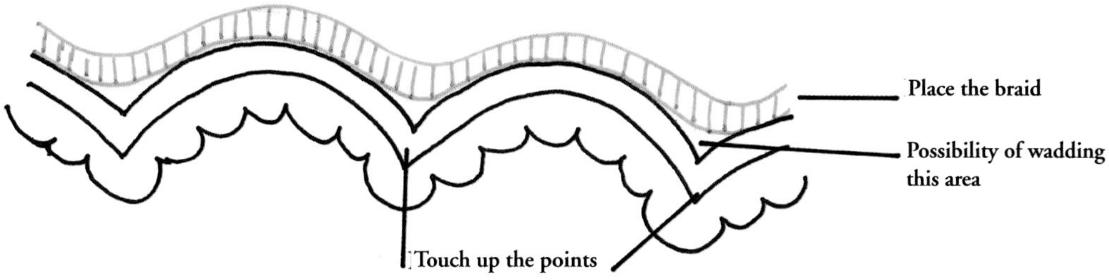

—— Place the braid

—— Possibility of wadding this area

Touch up the points

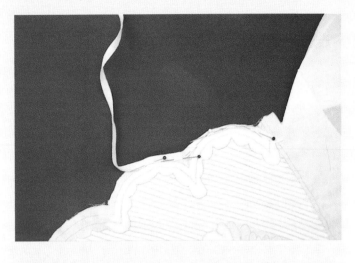

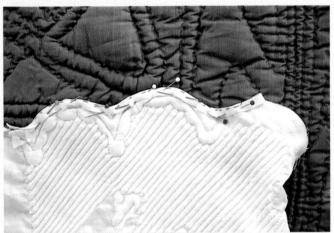

The different stages of placing a braid.

9. Finishing with blanket stitch

Blanket stitch is frequently found on old 'vanes', particularly on those that have ringed borders. In these cases, the lace is non-existent. (See diagram of stitches used.)

Characteristics of the stitch

There is only a height of 2 or 3 mm that is closely worked, like on buttonholes. The matt embroidery thread is twisted into a single strand, not polished.

In order to avoid the fabric folding whilst executing the stitch, here is a little trick:
– On the wrong side of the work, complete large tacking stitches on a straight piece of brown wrapping paper – only – on the part that is to be embroidered. (See photo.)

– The stitch is completed on the right side, having completed the rest of the stitching. It is advised to trace, beforehand, a line that is not to be passed: The stitching should be nothing but regular.
– The paper will hold the fabric well, and allows the execution of the stitch to be easier; it is enough to glide the needle between the fabric and the paper on the wrong side, then to remove the paper afterwards. Do not cut the border straight away, (see photograph.)

The work is now ready to be padded.

Once finished, the 'boutis' should be washed in cold water, then in warm water, wrung out and then dried.

Now you can proceed, with care, with cutting the border. **First of all, cut as much material off as you can, approaching the blanket stitch, then make a clean cut, with the help of small nail scissors, or small embroidery scissors.**

In the present day, it is possible to use either the braid or the blanket stitch to complete works of all sizes.

In a private collection, one of the last 'vanes' which had not been wadded, but on which the stitching had been finished, shows a festooned border, made with wooden stamps, ready for embroidery…

Certain 'vanes' of silk, with refined stitches, show rolled arches, stitched with hemstitch or with running stitch.

The 'bourrasses' or 'bourrassons' and quilted 'piqués' are finished with a tight hemstitch.

The embroidery cotton was matt, without shine.

Embroidery stitches are completed at the same time as stitching.

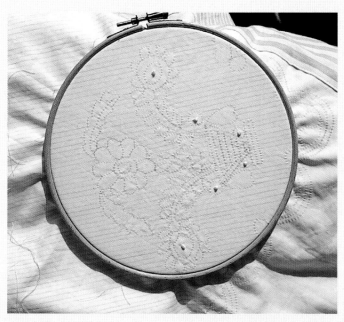

The blanket stitch is completed after the stitching stage.

Cutting the fabric is done after washing.

10. Transparency and relief

Transparency

Transparency is obtained by **not wadding certain carefully chosen areas.** It should place value on the motifs, give a style to the work, and give light to an ensemble, which appears over-charged.

The alternating parts, that are wadded or flat, cause some technical problems, as the fabric is at risk of buckling. In order to remedy this, here are a few suggestions, gleaned from old works, (our ancestors have already experimented and found the answers…)

– If you want a lot of transparency, choose a cotton fabric that is a little thicker than lawn.

– The wadding of the motifs should be lighter, (in the opposite, it will produce buckling.)

It is imperative that the fabric should be kept flat.

To achieve this there are several solutions:

– Stitch the whole piece: motifs, vermicelli, details… and only wad the areas that interest you.

– Use 'piqué de Marseille' or 'broderie de Marseille', (see later,) alternating with 'boutis'.

– Use a closed running stitch on the interior of a flower or a leaf.

– If the top of the bridal 'jupon' normally presents an important area of wadding, (three layers,) on those from Saint-Maximin, (Var), made in a convent, certain 'boutis' flowers are found in staggered rows in order for the fabric to keep its shape. This is quite rare, but merits notice.

In all cases, the start and the finish of the stitching are invisible: they were done… and are still done on the motifs to be wadded.

The combination of various techniques

It is not unusual to find these on the same work, the areas padded and quilted and done in 'boutis', (example: the flat area of a quilted 'courtepointe', central medallion, and borders embroidered in 'boutis'.)

For particularly rich creations, 'broderie de Marseille' brings a refined touch. On these creations it is not vain to say that perfection is at your fingertips…

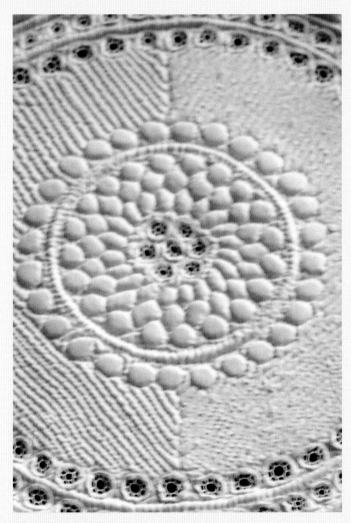

The alliance of 'broderie de Marseille' and of 'boutis'

Bridal 'jupon' in 'boutis', photographed showing its transparency.

Sculpting the fabric

The choice of motifs determines the quality of the relief.

- For a pronounced volume, it is necessary to force a number of tufts in, to the point where you feel that the fabric is at risk of tearing.
- Variations on the relief from one flower to the next, on the same type of flower, permit the fabric to be sculpted and bring to the fore certain motifs which hold particular meaning for you. Give a denser volume to a seed, to a pearl, by only passing the tuft through a few millimetres at the centre.
- The choice at the bottom, (vermicelli, squares…) is important, as it puts value on chosen ornaments, without stifling them. The base should give perspective to the work, placing value on those items that deserve it. Equally, it works together with the technique.

The area has taken its relief.

11. The 'piqué de Marseille'

This has no vermicelli or squares. It is confused, incorrectly, with quilting.

It is made up of floral motifs, closely leaved boughs, twined one within another. The ornaments are not out of depth with a base that is entirely done in 'boutis' and holds the fabric flat.

Transparency finds here a place of choice.

12. 'Broderie de Marseille'

On certain princely and noble clothing, this was in vogue, (it did not deign to be present on night caps…), it would fill the spaces between wadded motifs with stitches such as chain stitch and french knots… and proposes a different type of relief on the fabric. The 'broderie de Marseille' could adorn pearls and golden threads and also decorate quilting, for example, at the top of a bridal 'jupon'.

13. The role of colour

In the past, certain striped camisoles that were white, had tufts of indigo or pink. The colour of the tuft was only there to emphasise the beauty of a shape, or the purity of a line. On the other hand, there exist 'boutis' in yellow or blue silk.

In the present day, colour can be used to place value on a form, or to place shadow on a motif, but it should not overpower the 'boutis'. An extreme use of coloured tufts is not desirable. It is preferable to overtly work with coloured silk embroidery or with 'appliqué'.

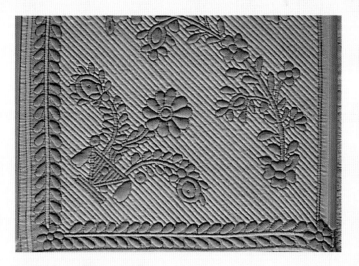

The colour emphasises the shapes.

14. Washing

Washing is done last, when the work is completely finished, even if that is a long wait, and even if your 'boutis' is grey with pencil and your finger marks.

A 'boutis' cannot be mistreated…

By hand

- The first wash is done **in cold water,** with 'savon de Marseille' in order to prevent the remains of the tracing (blue to yellow.)

- During the second wash, rub the grooves with the help of a soft brush, (an old toothbrush.) Rinse and **repeat.**
- In the case of marks, don't forget that 100% cotton can be boiled and supports light bleaching.
- Use whitener, (see instructions on the box.)
- Rinse several times **without ringing.**
- Roll between two bath towels.

In the machine

- Place your 'boutis' in a knotted pillowcase, or a little linen bag.
- Wash once in cold water, then a second time in a warm wash (around 40°…).
- Lay out, in the shade, flat, having reshaped the 'boutis' (pin out if necessary on a plank of wood covered in a towel). A long drying time is preferable.
- Cover it with a sheet as white attracts insects.

After the both wadding and washing stages, your 'boutis' will shrink by 10 to 15%. The wadding will settle, and its volume will appear smaller.

15. What to do with your pieces?

As in the past, give them as presents for births… marriages…

Modern life has diminished some women's spare time, and given it to others. Framing, placed as hangings, little pieces suit those who are working; the others are destined as never ending works, for those to whom time is of no issue.

A 'BOUTIS'
IS GIVEN,
IS ADMIRED,
LIVES,
IS TOUCHED…

Compositions and models

All the patterns (in real size) and models that are examined in this chapter are available in the booklet, *Le boutis dans le trousseau*, by Edisud. You can get it from the Edisud publishing house, at Aix-en-Provence, or from The Association 'Les Cordelles' at Calvisson or in certain specialised shops.

The models are unedited and original, specially chosen by the author for this book.

Complete beginners can start to learn on the simple motifs, (flower baskets, cornucopias, bunches of grapes and samplers of numbers and letters.) The baptism 'pétasson' will delight those with knowledge of the 'boutis'.

As to the most seasoned 'boutis' needlewomen, they could create a masterpiece with a 'vane', (or 'courtepointe') created by the author.

1. Basket of flowers

Let yourself be seduced by its simplicity and its elegance. The composition, sober and bare, places value on the stems, which, in their origin, were bordered in down, or present light swellings. The grace of the curves compensate for the more austere square pattern of the basket. The profile of the flowers forcefully emphasises the purity of the lines.

A bouquet of daisies and irises.
The daisy is the symbol of femininity and virginity.

Some advice for its creation

The stitching should be completed as indicated, from the centre towards the edge, as it pushes towards the sides.

– Stuff and wad.

– To please you, start by putting the flowers in 'boutis', (remember the pattern in order to respect the sense of direction of each tuft in each motif.)

The word 'tuft' specifically relates to the cotton that gives volume, used for stuffing. It is 100%, slightly twisted knitting cotton.

– If the petals are too long for your needle:

– Use the 'lasso' system…

– Or use a trapunto needle…

– Or, using a photocopier, reduce the motif by 80 or 90%

– Then, continue with the stalks with the help of a 'lasso'. In this way, work all of the gentle curves.

Remember: one passing of the tuft folded in two, (two strands in vermicelli,) 4 mm wide.

– Border the stems with their little lumps, which are wadded like petals.

– Then, start with the squares of the basket.

– Finally, sculpt the remaining little motifs, then start on the central vermicelli, (finish with the larger ones.)

– Complete the frame at the very end with the help of a 'lasso'. Pass through it twice and take care on the corners.

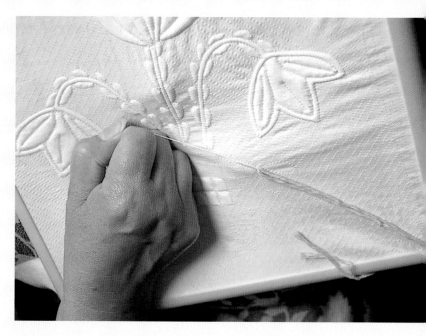

You must stitch in the same hole.

The entry of the tuft is a little delicate: it must stay in the vermicelli.

Repeat this procedure several times.

2. Bunch of grapes

Whether it be the Chasselas grapes that are round or the Muscat, with its oval grapes, the bunch of grapes is always sumptuously elegant. As the symbol of prosperity, it evokes the harvest. It is present on many works, including those dedicated to birth.

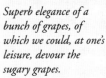

Superb elegance of a bunch of grapes, of which we could, at one's leisure, devour the sugary grapes.

Advice for completion

– Round and oval grapes are wadded in the same way: the stuffing should be forced. Don't fear pushing it in.

– Leave some transparency between the grapes; for that, complete your stitching, but don't wad it.

– The contour of the leaves may appear delicate; it isn't, because of the exiting tuft at each point. It will be necessary, in areas, to wad twice, (using the 'lasso' is not advised.)

– The leaves are wadded from the veins towards the points. They do not demand a rounded wadding, but a more flat one. When the relief is finished, pass a tuft the length of the vein, from one side to the other, to fill the empty spaces along the line of stitching.

– Tendrils are wadded in several goes.

– Once the technique has been assimilated, return to the grapes to give them a more rounded appearance, then to the leaves, to coddle the points.

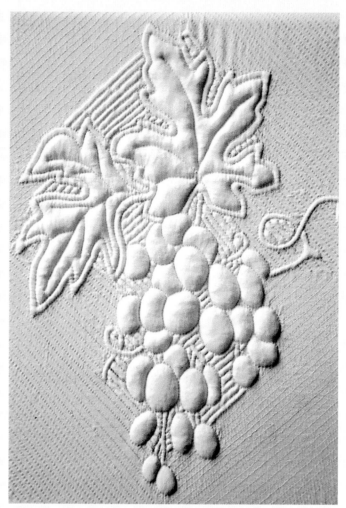

The progression of wadding is done in reference to the centre.

The stitching stage should be totally finished.

3. The cornucopia

Composed of flowers or fruits and sometimes both, it adorns, with a certain majesty, the central medallion of wedding 'courtepointes'. If it calls prosperity to the house of the young couple, it also invites them to create a solid family, with its basket (or vase) serving as an anchor in life.

The Medici vase that was in vogue in the time of Louis XIV, supports a composition where grace falls from one part and another, in fluid and generous movements.

*Symbols of prosperity and abundance,
flowers and fruits from Provence adorn the wedding 'courtepointes'.*

Advice For Its Completion

– There is no particular difficulty in its creation: all the shapes have been studied on patterns.

– The rings at the centre of the flowers can appear to be delicate to complete, but simple solutions appear on the patterns. At the worst, delete them, you will have a larger heart…

– Create some sculpture effects from one flower to another. Modify the relief by wadding one more in relation to another, or one part of a flower more than the rest. You will give depth to the scene.

– Petals of the left hand flower, (with its specific stamens which spurt out in gracious curves,) can be wadded with the 'lasso' on the condition that the tuft is interrupted at the end of each ring.

– **For wadding of flowers, cherries or pearls, it is not necessary to wad the hearts or seeds all in the same direction…**

It is in the motif itself where the sense of direction should be respected in order to prevent the tufts crossing.

– Its possible to leave transparency in the vase, between the stalks of the cherries and the leaves.

– This composition, enlarged on a photocopier, and enriched with other flowers or fruits, (see the booklet of drawings and the chapter on motifs,) can be used to create a beautiful central medallion for a work of a larger size.

– If you decide to frame your 'boutis', it is necessary to wad the borders in order to facilitate the techniques of completion on the work. The framer, or yourself, will find it easier hiding those vermicelli with an inner frame or a wooden frame.

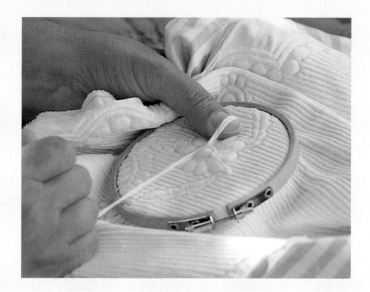

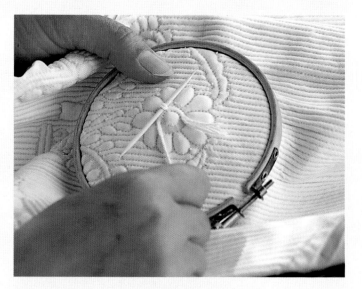

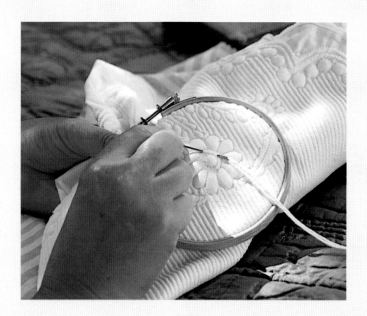

A few tricks to avoid the formation of knots and the lifting of the fabric.

174

4. The christening 'pétasson'

It is a love of the 'pétasson', an exquisite harmony, with all its finesse of delicate motifs, of eglantines and tulips.

The design has not been modified in its composition, as its balance is perfect.

To be given or to have received this precious work, with its delicate flowers, would then elegantly adorn a highly polished old piece of furniture, a low table, or an old wall painted in the colours of the South.

It would also add a refined touch to a contemporary environment. It is a creation which can be considered as a picture, but also guards its meaning in accompanying the new-born during its childhood.

The magic of a refined design.

Advice for the creation of the 'pétasson'

At the start, the fabric should not be washed.

The drawing takes account of approximately 10% shrinkage, due to the completion of the work. It is not necessary, therefore, to enlarge it.

Carefully copy the drawing, as indicated in the chapter 'Initiation to the 'Boutis'. If you do not have the use of a table for several hours, use a large piece of flat cardboard, (for example, a calendar,) or a board.

You can choose the border of the 'pétasson' between:
– A 'broderie anglaise' lightly folded.
– A finish in hemming stitch, which will give a bubbled effect to the last vermicelli.
– A different the border: festoons, (see the chapter on 'Finishing Touches')

Different possible compositions of the 'pétasson' starting from the proposed initial model

– Reproduce an identical bouquet in each of the four corners, (there are two proposed choices as there are two models.)
– Keep two baskets from the model vis à vis in two corners, and place your initials vis à vis in the other two corners.
– Keep the heart and the baskets, remove the wreath of roses, and gently advance the star anise flowers.
– Remove the heart and place at the centre of a star anise flower.
– Place the daisies from the bouquets in place of the star anise flowers and vice versa.
– Compartmentalise the interior of the baskets, in little squares or little lozenges.
– Choose other baskets from the models in the initiation section. You could, for example, enlarge or reduce the baskets, the flowers from the 'vane' as well as the sampler.

In the past, they did not give regard to the scale of the motifs.

In the present day, using a photocopier let us balance the size within the composition.

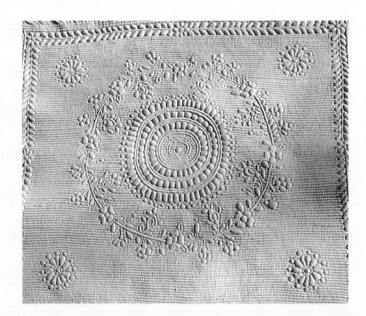

Buttons of roses and light flowers of eglantine, for the springtime of one's life.

175

CHRISTENING PÉTASSON

Order of Wadding:

1. The central circle.
2. The small central vermicelli.
3. The rings, (to be completed in several stages, that is to say, at least five. Cut the tuft each time you exit. See the initiation pattern)
4. Vermicelli around the rings.

It is possible to tuft them in the following order, 1, 3, 2, 4.

Exit point of the tufts.

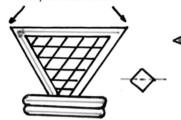

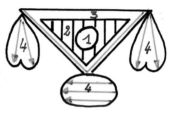

Put the finishing touches to the points by wadding with double thread, close to the edge. Exit at the point.

Passing the thread through each little lozenge once, (the tuft is doubled.) Leave 5 mm of cotton outside the entrance and the exit point, and push in, so that none can come back out. Continue in this way for each of the small motifs.

Always start at the interior of the motif. Order of stuffing, 1, 2, 3, 4.

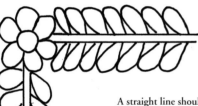

A straight line should be completed in one go if possible. Calculate the length of cotton to use. Use the 'lasso' either with a tapestry needle or with a trapunto needle.

For vermicelli that are 5 mm wide, (the frame,) pass two strands through twice.
In the corners, leave 5 mm outside, cut, push in the surplus which will complete the angle neatly.
As you need, add a little cotton,
(on the exterior angle – see the sheet on perfecting your wadding.)

Festoons are wadded last.
Firstly, the bottom scallop,
then the second, upper scallop.
In the festoon, the cotton descends towards the base.
Therefore, start towards the bottom. Pass the doubled thread through several times with the 'lasso'.
Then complete every little cavity.
Proceed in the same way for the second scallop.
If necessary, add a little bit of cotton in the points.

5. A masterpiece… The wedding 'vane' embroidered from the inside in 'boutis'

This wedding 'vane', (or 'courtepointe') has been elaborated on after the rules of the traditional composition, with motifs and symbols from the Provençal pictoral repertoire.

A masterpiece to be embroidered, to be given and to be admired, so that it enchants others, and "enchants oneself". (Socrates.)

The 'vane' (or 'courtepointe') is a lifelong masterpiece. Like Mira and Albertine, be quite bold in throwing yourself into a creation in which time is of no importance, where each season leaves its own imprint. Give yourself the freedom to explore your imagination; whilst respecting the proposed composition, give it your personal touch. If the straight border appears too sober for you, adopt the scallops of the 'pétasson' and join it with flowers…

WEDDING 'VANE'

Work using 'piqué de Marseille' between the large motifs.

Direction of wadding for the large motifs.

Leave some transparency in the centre around the seeds.

SUGGESTIONS

Possibility of varying the direction of the vermicelli

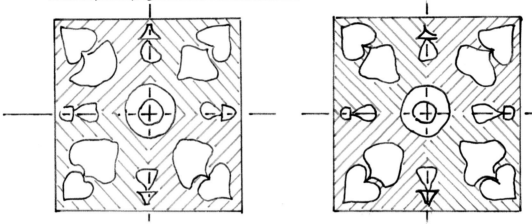

Vermicelli in lozenges.

Vermicelli in a star shape.

Wadding of the baskets

There are several possibilities:

– Complete wadding.
– Only wadding the squares.
– Only wadding the lines.

– Wadding one vermicelli in two.

Light wadding

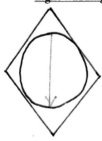

The effect of a pastel is obtained by not wadding the whole surface.
The tuft is introduced following the diagrammatical example shown.
At the entrance and exit, leave 1 cm or more of cotton.
Push it in with a cocktail stick.

Diagram for the tuft.

Advice for completing the 'vane'

At the beginning, the fabric should not be washed.

The pattern of the 'vane' measures 1.6 metres on each side; you will need two lots of fabric of this dimension or larger. Avoid, at all cost, linking stitches, which will make the passing of the tufts difficult.

It is necessary to have 20 cm of fabric around the design. If you don't have them, place extra bands of fabric around, ('chutes'.) Combed cottons from Egypt, that are found in shops, are sufficiently wide.

You could fold the fabric in two, in which case you would have the same material on top and underneath.

You could choose a cotton lawn for the top, and use a combed Egyptian cotton for the underneath. Whatever the cotton fabric chosen, it should be fine, 100% cotton, and it must not have been washed.

Trial soak the cotton thread and the wadding, in order to refine your judgement. A sample lets you test the materials.

A cotton cloth should be easy to stitch for the first five minutes, but at the end of two hours of stitching, the wrist and fingers become tired.

On a 'boutis', the colour white dominates 90%, but there also is 10% colour, divided between sunflower yellow and the Provençal blue. Also there was green or salmon pink, (for certain works created in silk.)

If you choose silk, do not use raw silk. Crucially, the underside should be made of cotton, of lawn, of one type, co-ordinated with the top.

Your thread should be the same colour as the top fabric.

Transferring the design to the 'vane' takes time, method and patience. It is worthwhile to look at the advice relative to the transfer of the design. Don't forget your perpendicular lines, to be traced in crayon from the beginning.

The sheet of vermicelli can be transferred, quarter by quarter, in the direction that you have chosen.

The perpendicular lines are important guidelines. They help with the order: the design of the central motif, then the corners, corner by corner, the bouquets situated on the sides, then the vermicelli.

Several combinations for the bottom are possible, (see the diagram to the left.) Whatever your choice, make sure that your joins for the vermicelli are good, when you transfer your pattern. If the lines do not coincide, you will be able to rectify this whilst stitching, as long as the discrepancy is minimal. The plate of vermicelli proposes intervals of 4 mm, which is the most refined, emphasising the elegance of the ensemble and only requires passing the tuft through once, (the cotton should be double.)

In the central crown, the vermicelli are in the warp.

A bulbous heart, chiselled in the 'boutis',
a bouquet blooms from a jet of water on the fabric;
flowers and seeds celebrate nature.

Choice of fine fabrics

If you are using lawn, or cotton fabrics that are particularly fine, it is necessary to add the motifs to be stitched in the central medallion, in order to keep a level surface for when the 'boutis' will be finished.

These motifs may already have been used between different flowers. This stitching supplementation may be made up of pearls and lines… or other forms in harmony with the ensemble, (for example, the seeds aligned towards the centre of the fruit.) It should have been predetermined from the beginning, and should be done before the wadding.

This procedure was used by the 'boutis' needlewomen.

Different possible compositions of the 'vane'

– Reproduce the same bouquet in the four corners, (two solutions of your choice.)

– Having looked at the proposed model for the 'vane', modify:

The order of the flowers or choose only one type. Remove the leafy garland and replace regularly with a flower from the bouquet, (repeat several times.) Modify the border. Change the centre, in using that of the 'pétasson'. Remove the little bouquets from the middle and choose motifs, (hearts, for example,) and enlarge according to your taste. The motifs should be identical from side to side.

Place your initials in the centre of the medallions that you have placed in the borders, as well as the year.

Respect the rules of the composition.

The quality of the technique depends on this.

Problems and solutions

1. Stitching

Irregular stitches

– There is no secret… stitching will improve with practice.

– With each length of thread, take care at the beginning and do three or four stitches at a time; start again, applying yourself and be determined to succeed.

– Bring the needle back and redo your stitches immediately.

Oversized stitches

– As soon as you see the point of the needle shine, stitch immediately in order to shorten the following stitch.

– Take a smaller needle, (number 10 and then a number 12 for the more experienced amongst you.)

– Each time the thread exits, hold it on the work with the little finger of your right hand, before starting on a new series of stitches.

The back has not been properly taken

– At the beginning, turn your work over often in order to check it; as you need, complete a larger stitch on the back.

– To undo the thread is not easy… do not stitch twice on the same line. The moment you make a mistake it must be rectified.

– Push your needle through at right angles to the fabric and bring it back up, catching the two layers properly.

Exposed knots

– Enter the work "the wrong way". Do not let the knot stick against the line of stitching… hold it with your left hand before blocking it with a backstitch.

– When you need to, make no more knots: start the line of stitching with a backstitch, having left a good length of thread, (1 or 2 cm) on the inside… Finish in the same way.

– **Know that you can wait until it has been wadded to correct the fault.** When the motif has been wadded or padded, take a new cocktail stick, push the knot through its exit hole… twist it… once it is inside, move it further in. The wadding will block its exit.

Using a hoop

– Practice 5 minutes every day in order to become used to it. Choose the smallest, (10 cm in diameter,) for motifs… it is easy to hold, manipulate and can be easily adjusted. It contributes to the quality of the work.

Then change from diameter to diameter, depending on your need.

"I've pricked my finger"

– Protect it… or, if you prefer to have contact with the fabric, place your middle finger of your left hand on the vertical – in particular the nail – your finger will butt up against it.

– A little bit of saliva will remove a blood mark (!)… whilst waiting to be washed.

2. Wadding and padding

Buckling on the right side
– Stitches have jumped during the wadding stage.
– The wrong side has not been picked up properly, your stitch is too small.
– The cotton tuft is too fat, (double check its size.).

The thickness of the vermicelli
– 4 mm in width, one passing, (two strands,) is sufficient.
– 5 mm in width, it is possible to pass the wadding through twice… or choose a thicker cotton.

Granules in the wadding
– You are cutting your tuft too long. There is too much cotton to push in.
– You are pushing your cotton too far.
– Whilst passing the second layer through, stay close to the surface and hold the motif with your fingers whilst passing the tuft through.
Any correction to be made is done on the right side. Move the cotton through with a cocktail stick.

The tuft is getting rolled up in the vermicelli
– It is getting too warm: you are using too long a tuft.
– Before passing it through, smooth out your strands.
– Watch it carefully whilst you are passing it through… intervene immediately: pull it back… and go slower.
– If you have oversized stitches, the tuft will try to get out between the stitches and will take on a meandering aspect… not disagreeable!

The tuft is puckering in a motif
– There is trapped air… its normal, especially for the first few tufts!
– You are cutting your tuft too long. As a consequence, when pushing it in, it puckers.

'Boudifle' at the end of your vermicelli
– You are cutting the tuft too long and you are pushing it too far with the cocktail stick.
– Correct it, on the right side, by pushing the cotton further down with the cocktail stick.

Appreciating the wadding
– Between two fingers, the wadding should be solid; the surface of the fabric should be smooth and stretched… there should be no creases.

– It is always possible to wad again, sometimes even after it has been washed.

The work is deformed
– Look again at the order of completion in the stitching… use tighter tacking stitches.
– You must wait until the whole surface has been wadded before judging it.
– From time to time, put the work back into place by pulling on the warp; having washed, pull it back into shape.

The tuft is coming out of the motif
– Your stitch is too large. If the needle crosses the stitching, stop at a sensible point. Do as if…

Holes on the wrong side
– Your tuft should be in the extension of the needle.
– Use the 'lasso' more often.
– Push out the fibres of the fabric in order to push it into place.
– Your cotton is of a large calibre.
– Your cocktail stick is too big… use a smaller cocktail stick.
– Push in the tuft with great care…

Areas where cotton is missing
– Add cotton wherever you want!
– If your work is stretched on a hoop or frame, you should not be missing anything at the end of a vermicelli… if, however, this happens, don't cut the tuft so short.

I've cut the fabric!
– Whilst cutting the mesh, rectify it on the vertical, and hold the pair of scissors parallel to the fabric.
– Use little nail scissors that are curved at the top.
– On the wrong side, repair it with a little stitch, for example, a blind hemstitch.
– On the right side, you will have to innovate…! Put in an embroidery stitch… and repeat it… or stitch on a patch of identical fabric.

ENJOY LEARNING TO 'BOUTIS' MY FRIENDS!

Dictionary

Arch. Dép. – Country archives.

Aune – Measure of length that was used at that time.

Basin or Bazin – Mixed fabric which must be made with linen and cotton, with as much in the warp as in the weft.

Bastide – Large low buildings surrounded by vines. Owned by the 'bastidan'.

Batiste – Very fine linen, and very soft, squarely woven. It gets its name from its inventor, Jean Baptiste, a weaver from Cambrai. Used mainly in underwear, it has a slight sheen.

Bourre – wadding/ flock. Raw, woolly and unspun.

Bourrasse – wadding.

Bourrasson/Culachon – A quilted piece about 50 cm x 50 cm of fairly ordinary stitching, put under the baby's bottom.

Bourrette – see Filoselle

Boutisser – verb for making a 'boutis'. Boutisseuse – person who makes the 'boutis'.

Cache-brassière – item of clothing used to hide the shirt of the new-born.

Cache-maillot – item of clothing used to hide that swaddling bands.

Cadis - Type of cheap woollen cloth that the peasants used to make clothes.

Calicot - From Calcutta, Indian port on the Malabar Coast. Used for printed calico.

Camelot - Thick silk or wool cloth or camel or goat hair. Mix of silk and angora.

Chauffoir – Small pieces of 'boutis' sewn in vermicelli that were warmed in the fire place and used for warming a chilled person. It is also said that they were placed on the stomachs of a pregnant during birth.

Cotillons – Petticoat or underskirt.

Cotonnine – Light cotton fabric. Also used to make heavy fabric where the warp was of cotton and the weft of hemp – used for boat sails.

Coton – Fluffy down, long and fine, from which cotton was taken.

Courtepointe – Counterpane.

Coussinière – These were covers or small pillowcases that hid a cushion.

Couverte/Couverture – Bedspread.

Couverton – Small bedspread.

Couvre-pieds/couvre pates – foot cover.

Filoselle/Filoseille/Filozelle – silk flock/wadding, used to make fabrics and stockings.

Futaine – Old fabric of thick cotton.

Jupon – Underskirt.

Lizat – A fine quality white cotton fabric from India, and which was used for making stitched bedspreads in Marseilles.

Mas – large farmhouse found in the Midi.

Nankin – Cotton or yellow silk fabric imported from China from its namesake.

Percale – Originally Indian, the word means 'very fine fabric'. It comes from Pondichery.

Pétasson – Square of 'boutis'.

Piqueuses – Person who makes a 'piqué'.

Poncif – Perforated design: the outline of the pattern was pierced with small holes, letting the marking chalk through.

Rouennerie – (Rouen, Rouan) Cotton fabric of a lower quality.

Vane – counterpane coming from the Provencal word 'vano'. In many old inventories the word is written 'vanne'. It was a 'courtepointe' which did not cover the whole bed.

Vano/Vanon – small counterpane.

Bibliography

Grand dictionnaire des symboles et des mythes, Nadia Julien, Marabout.

Dictionnaire des symboles, Jean Chevalier - Alain Gheerbrant, Éditions Laffont Jupiter.

Dictionnaire Quillet de la langue française.

La flore sculptée dans l'art médiéval, Ana Maria de Quinonès, Éditions Desclée de Brouwer.

Dictionnaire des représentations et croyances en Occident, Xosé Ramon Marino Ferro, Éditions Desclée de Brouwer.

Dentelles l'Aventurine, Paris 1995.

Les papiers peints en arabesques, Collection Artémuse, Patrimoine Éditions de la Martinière, ouvrage sous la direction de Bernard Jacqué.

Rosalie, Léa, Emélie, Éva et les autres Femmes de la Vaunage au XIXᵉ siècle, H.B. Éditions 1997. Éd. de la Vaunage.

Livre en broderie. Reliures françaises du Moyen Âge à nos jours, Bibliothèque Nationale de France.

Les tapisseries coptes du musée historique des tissus, Yvonne Bourgon-Amir, Publications de la recherche. Université de Montpellier, Tome 1 - Tome 2. 1993.

Syrie - Signes d'étoffe, Maison des cultures du monde, A.C.L. Édition 1988-Société Crocus.

La Route des Indes, Catalogue d'exposition, Musée des Arts Décoratifs d'Aquitaine, Bordeaux 1988, SOMOGY, Éditions d'ART.

Au royaume du signe, Fondation Dapper 1988, ADAM BIRO.

Histoire de la Provence, Maurice Agulhon - Noël Coulet, Éditions ?

Le Languedoc pour héritage, André Soulier, Presses du Languedoc.

Histoire du Languedoc, sous la direction de Philippe Wolff, Privat.

Le roman de Tristan et Iseult, Joseph Bédier, Union générale d'Éditions.

La mémoire de l'humanité Les grands explorateurs, Sous la direction de Nadeije Laneyrie-Dagen.

Les seigneurs de la soie. Trois siècles d'une famille cévenole, (XVIᵉ - XIXᵉ), Jean-Paul Chabrol, Presses du Languedoc.

Nos garrigues et les Assemblées au désert, Docteur Albert Domergue - Presses du Languedoc, Max Chaleil, Éditeur.

L'île de Camargue. Histoire d'un pays singulier, Clément Martin, Presses du Languedoc. Max Chaleil, Éditeur, Camargue.

Histoire de France. À propos d'un Édit Royal : celui de Nantes avril 1598, Conférence de Pierre Fanguin, Professeur agrégé Honoraire.

Historique de l'Occitanie, André Dupuy - avec la collaboration de Marcel Carrière et André Nouvel, Collection Connaissance de l'Occitanie, Éditions Assimil.

Andrinople. Le rouge magnifique. De la teinture à l'impression, une cotonnade à la conquête du monde, Collection Artémuse, Patrimoine Éditions de la Martinière.

Le costume populaire provençal, Rode de basso Prouvenço, Musée des Arts et Traditions Populaires de moyenne Provence, Édisud.

Encyclopédie des ouvrages de dames, T. de Dillmont.

La broderie du XIᵉ siècle jusqu'à nos jours, L. de Farcy. Angers 1870.

L'art du brodeur, Charles Germain de Saint-Aubin. Paris 1770

Charles de Baschi, Marquis d'Aubais, Mathias Baron Martel (Inventaire 1776), Arch. dép. du Gard 1996.

En jupon piqué et robe d'indienne, Michel Biehn, Édit. Jeanne Laffite - 1987.

Histoire du costume d'Arles, Odile et Magali Pascal, Auto-Éditeur.

Lou vèsti prouvençau, Nougier Simone et Estelle - 1980, Auto-éditeur.

Guide de la flore méditerranéenne, Ingrid et Peter Schonfelder, Hatier.

Le guide des fleurs sauvages, R. Fitter - A. Fitter - M. Blamey, Delachaux et Niestle.

L'histoire du costume, François Boucher, Flammarion.

Circulades languedociennes de l'an mille, Krzysztof Pawlowski, Presses du Languedoc.

Abécédaire des pratiques vestimentaires en France de 1780 à 1800, Nicole Pellegrin, Édition Alinéa.

La terre des femmes et ses magies, Jocelyne Bonnet, Édit. Robert Laffont.

La gravure de mode féminine en France, Raymond Gaudriault, Les Éditions de l'Amateur.

Le boutis, ouvrage divin, Dominique Le Roux, Auto-éditeur.

Le textile en Provence, Annie Roux, Édisud.

Les arts décoratifs en Provence du XVIIᵉ au XIXᵉ siècle, M.-J. Beaumelle - G. & V. Guerre - P. Jacquenoud, Édisud.

Quilts of Provence. The Art and craft of French Quiltmaking, Berenson Kathryn, New York, Archetype Press Book, Henry Holt and compagny, 1996

Le Boutis, Solange Kergreis, éditions Didier Carpentier.

Manuel du boutis, Andrée Gaussens, éditions La bibliothèque des Métiers.

List of lenders

- Association Les Cordelles . . . . .Calvisson - Gard
- Mr Cabanel André Jean . . . . .Aujargues - Gard
- Mr Caritey . . . . .Montpellier - Hérault
- Mrs C… . . . . .Bernis - Gard
- Mrs D… . . . . .La Rouvière - Gard
- Mrs G… . . . . .Saint Dionizy - Gard
- Mrs G… . . . . .Souvignargues - Gard
- Mrs L… . . . . .Marsillargues - Hérault
- Mrs M… . . . . .Bernis - Gard
- Mrs Moysan . . . . .Marsillargues - Hérault
- Mrs N… . . . . .Calvisson - Gard
- Mrs O… . . . . .Calvisson - Gard
- Mrs Peytier . . . . .Lyon
- Mrs P… . . . . .Aimargues - Gard
- Mrs R… . . . . .Congénies - Gard
- Mrs Roussel . . . . .Mus - Gard
- Mrs Rouvin Lyse . . . . .Beauvoisin - Gard
- Mrs R… . . . . .Marsillargues - Hérault
- Mrs Gosse . . . . .Paris
- Mrs A… . . . . .Aspères - Gard

as well as all those listed in the collection.

STUDIED COLLECTIONS

The pieces of 'boutis' studied have all come from private collections. Therefore, all copies or photocopies of these works are strictly forbidden.

PILLOWCASES EMBROIDERED WITH 'BOUTIS'

- Pillowcase for a child . . . . .Collection Moysan
- Pillowcase for a child . . . . .Aspères (Gard)
- Pillowcase for a child . . . . .Association Les Cordelles - Calvisson
- Pillowcase with birds . . . . .Calvisson (Gard) - Collection privée
- Pillowcase with a central rose . . . . .Collection Moysan
- Pillowcase with bunches of grapes . . . . .Collection Moysan
- Pillowcase . . . . .Madame Peytier originally from Beauvoisin (Gard)
- Pillowcase with palmettes . . . . .Collection A.J. Cabanel
- Cushion cover . . . . .Madame Rouvin Lyse - Beauvoisin
- Cushion cover . . . . .Madame P… - Aimargues.

PÉTASSONS EMBROIDERED IN 'BOUTIS'

- Pétasson . . . . .Madame Gavalda – originally from Marseilles
- Pétasson . . . . .Collection Moysan - originally from Aix en Provence
- Pétasson with five pointed star . . . . .Association Les Cordelles - originally from Marseilles
- Pétasson bunches of grapes . . . . .Association Les Cordelles - originally from Provence
- Pétasson with adiamond shaped star . . . . .Association Les Cordelles - originally from Provence
- Pétasson from Arles . . . . .Collection Nicolle
- Pétasson from Nîmes . . . . .Association Les Cordelles
- Pétasson with leaves + bunches of grapes . . . . .Association Les Cordelles - originally from Aubagne
- Pétasson with five flowers . . . . .Association Les Cordelles - originally from Provence
- Pétasson with hearts . . . . .Association Les Cordelles - originally from Provence
- Pétasson centre + flowering stems . . . . .Association Les Cordelles - originally from Provence
- Pétasson with star + garland of leaves . . . . .Association Les Cordelles - originally from Provence
- Bourrasson (wadded) . . . . .Madame Gavalda - Marseilles
- Bourrasson (wadded) . . . . .Madame Gavalda – Marseilles

WHITE 'VANES' EMBROIDERED IN 'BOUTIS'

- Vane with mimosas . . . . .Collection Moysan - Marsillargues
- Vane with mimosas . . . . .Madame Raï - originally from Marsillargues
- Vane with a flowering sun . . . . .Collection Moysan - Marsillargues
- Vane with a flowering sun . . . . .Madame Rouvin Lyse-Beauvoisin
- Vane with cauldron . . . . .Madame Lamazère - Marsillargues
- Vane with cauldron . . . . .Collection Moysan - Marsillargues
- Vane in vermicelli . . . . .Madame Roussel - Mus
- Vane (reconstructed) . . . . .Collection Moysan - Marsillargues
- Vane with fans . . . . .Madame Peytier - Beauvoisin
- Vane belonging to Albertine . . . . .Madame Bouad - Aimargues
- Vane with palmettes . . . . .Collection A.J. Cabanel
- Vane with bouquets . . . . .Collection A.J. Cabanel
- Vane with pomegranates . . . . .Association Les Cordelles - Calvisson
- Vane with bouquets and a central medallion . . . . .Association Les Cordelles - Calvisson
- Vane with wadded main area bordered in 'boutis' . . . . .Collection A.J. Cabanel
- Vane with people . . . . .Collection Moysan
- Vane with symbols . . . . .Madame Caritey - Montpellier
                                                                                  - originally from Provence
- Vane with vermicelli 17th century . . . . .Madame Renée Gosse – Paris

Coloured 'vanes' embroidered in 'boutis':
- Vane of blue silk . . . . .Collection R... - Congénies
- Vane of yellow silk . . . . .Collection P... - Saint Mamert.

VANONS EMBROIDERED IN 'BOUTIS'

- Vanon . . . . .Madame Rouvin Lyse - Beauvoisin
- Vanon . . . . .Madame Peytier - Beauvoisin
- Vanon with birds . . . . .Collection A.J. Cabanel
- Vanon with central medallion . . . . .Collection Moysan
- Vanon in machine stitching . . . . .Collection O… - Calvisson
- Vanon in machine stitching . . . . .Madame Rouvin Lyse - Beauvoisin

BRIDAL 'JUPONS' (UNDERSKIRTS) EMBROIDERED IN 'BOUTIS'

- Bridal 'jupon' . . . . .Association Les Cordelles - Calvisson
- Bridal 'jupon' . . . . .Association Les Cordelles - Calvisson
- Bridal 'jupon' . . . . .Collection N. - Calvisson
- Bridal 'jupon' (1780) . . . . .Madame Coquillat - Meyreuil - B. du Rhône
- Bridal 'jupon' . . . . .Collection Moysan - Marsillargues
- Bridal 'jupon' . . . . .Collection Rouvin Lyse - Beauvoisin
- Bridal 'jupon' (1845) . . . . .Collection A.J. Cabanel
- Bridal 'jupon' . . . . .Collection A.J. Cabanel.
- Bridal 'jupon' with flowers . . . . .Collection S. Faa - Fuveau - B. du Rhône
- Bridal 'jupon' having belonged to . . . . .Belina Duverdier - Collection Mme Bain
                                                                                                    - Saint Tropez

'JUPONS' STITCHED AND WADDED

- 'Jupon' stitched with black silk . . . . .Clarensac - Madame V.
- Bridal white 'jupon' . . . . .Association Les Cordelles - Calvisson
- Beige 'jupon' with white motifs, 2.60m in length,
  9 vermicelli, stitched flowers, in florets .Collection C. Paul - Meyreuil (B. du Rhône)
- Blue 'jupon' 2.60m in length 15 close vermicelli . . . . .Collection C. Paul - Meyreuil
- Printed calico 'jupon' 17 vermicelli going this way and that . . . . .Collection Coquillat - Meyreuil
- Jupon with flowers (pomegranate flowers) 2.68m in length,
  14 vermicelli . . . . .Collection C. Paul
- Jupon maroon borders, 2.60m in length .Collection S. Faa - Fuveau
- Red 'jupon' with little blue flowers . . . . .Association Les Cordelles - Calvisson
- Beige 'jupon' with little flowers . . . . .Association Les Cordelles – Calvisson

OTHER PIECES IN 'BOUTIS'

- Cradle cover with hydrangeas . . . . .Collection Moysan
- Cradle cover . . . . .Collection Moysan
- Armchair covering . . . . .Madame P… - Aimargues
- Reconstructed 'vane' from a 'jupon' and from pieces of 'boutis' . . . . .Madame D… - La Rouvière

WADDED SILK 'VANES'

- Vane in yellow silk . . . . .Madame M... - Bernis
- Vane in yellow silk . . . . .Madame C... - Bernis
- Vane in blue silk . . . . .Mademoiselle G... - Souvignargues
- White wedding vane . . . . .Madame N... - Calvisson
- Vane in blue silk . . . . .Madame D... - Langlade
- Vane in greyish - blue silk . . . . .Madame R... - Congénies
- Vane in yellow silk . . . . .Madame D... - La Rouvière
- Vane in silk of brown monochrome . . . . .Clarensac - Madame A.

'COUVERTURES' STITCHED (WADDED) IN COTTON

- Couverton in white 'basin' . . . . .Madame Caritey - Montpellier
- Couverton in white 'basin' . . . . .Madame Caritey - Montpellier
- 4 printed calico 'couvertures' . . . . .Madame R... - Congénies
- 'Couverture' in toile de Jouy (biblical scenes) . . . . .Madame D... - La Rouvière
- Couverture of printed calico . . . . .Madame D... - La Rouvière
- Couverture of printed calico . . . . .Association Les Cordelles - Calvisson
- Couvertures of printed calicos . . . . .Collection A.J. Cabanel.

Work boxes shown are of the period.
- work box in solid ivory Louis Philippe
- Travel companion box Napoléon III
- Red work box beginning of the 19th century
Private shop collection : Broderie du Garlaban - 4, rue Mireille - Aubagne
Kind participation of the Maison Lebeaufil - 50, rue Gal. Chanzy - Roubaix

La Maison du Boutis

30420 Calvisson

Opened from 01/05 to 31/10 : thirsdays, fridays, saturdays, sundays from 2.30 p.m. up to 6 p.m. ; and from 01/11 to 30/04 : fridays, saturdays, sundays from 2.30 p.m. up to 6 p.m.
Closed on mondays and work holidays and from 15/12 to 31/01.
For all informations, fone to 04 66 01 63 75

Thanks

During the years of research, many people have helped and supported me, putting collections of precious boutis at my disposition or opening their doors to me. The encouragements and the tokens of sympathy have helped me to keep going throughout this long-term affair.

All actions undertaken surrounding this project would not have materialized without the participation of the unknown boutis creators as well as those of the Cordelles…and their husbands!

I address this to all, with my warmest thanks, in particular those with their clarifying advice and their open ears:

Jocelyne BONNET, professor of Ethnology – Université Montpellier III

Monsieur ROGER Jean-Marc, of the Académie de Nîmes

Monsieur LUCE, National President of the Foyers Ruraux de France

Monsieur FATTORI, curator of the Musée des Arts and Traditions Populaires de Moyenne Provençe at Draguignan and Madame ALBRAN

Madame SERENA-ALLIER, curator of the Museon Arlaten at Arles (Museum of ethnology)

Monsieur TRAVIER Daniel, curator of the Musée des Vallées Cévenoles at Saint-Jean-du-Gard

Monsieur PUECH, curator of the Musée Arts et Traditions in Le Vigan

Madame VERDIER Renée, my "folklore god-mother"

Monsieur CABANEL André-Jean, collector

Madame MOYSAN, collector

Messieurs LEPETZ Patrick, from Sauve and COMBE Jean-Marie, from Novezan-Venterol, artists/painters,

Whose friendly workshops have served as backgrounds to certain photographs of 'boutis'

Madame GRELICHE, National President of 'Patchwork Français'

A thousand thanks to Mesdames MEON Mireille, MONTREDON Danièle, GEOFFROY Chantal,

to Messieurs FOULQUIER, passionate botanist, PEYRIC Yves, ORTIZ Laurent, ORTIZ Tristan, LEPOUTRE Bernard (Lebaufil cotton)

to Madame and Monsieur ROCHE,

to Mesdames PAUL, COQUILLAT, FAA.

Mesdames GREGGIO and STRANGWAYS-PIZZOLI, AUBERT

Amongst the light fingers of the association "Les Cordelles, Boutis en Vaunage", those of Mesdames BERGOGNE Victoria, BLIN Joëlle, COLLIER Arlette, DAYCARD Gina, DIVOL Monique, GOMIS Danielle, ISCACHE Danièle, JULIEN-BAYLE Suzy, LEBRUN Armande, LEPERE Jeannine, NADOBNY Françoise, NICOLAS Geneviève, NICOLLE Agathe, NOURRIT Cosette, RONDEAUX Andrée, ROUSSEL Jacqueline, SORIANO Myriam, THURIN Isabelle, VIALA Monique and the author have participated, with enthusiasm, to the creation of the 'boutis'.

The relief and the transparence of the 'boutis' were photographed by Jean-Louis AUBERT,
who, with talent, knew how to tame during the different seasons, the changing of the shadows and the caprices of the sun.

The cartographical reconstructions are by Sadik FARABI.

The photographs on pages 12, 28, 57 n° 2, 3, 4, 59, are by Max Sagon.

The diagrams that appear in the book as well as those shown in the pocket collection 'Le boutis dans le trousseau' which complete the practical section of the book, were put together and remodelled by Isabelle THURIN, from the drawings by Francine NICOLLE, copied from old 'boutis' belonging to her. The composition of the 'vane' is from the author, from motifs in her collection; the creation of the bouquets and the drawing in real size is thanks to Isabelle THURIN.

The photographs on the cover of the pocket collection 'Le boutis dans le trousseau' are by Jean-Louis AUBERT.

Last, but by no means least, I thank my husband, for the patience that he has shown over the years and for his efficiency "in front of the computer…", to my three "ic", Dominique Tutin, Eric and Patrick Nicolle, to my granddaughters, 'boutisseuses' of tomorrow, for their care and thoughts at all times.

Contents list